Awakening
the workplace

Achieving Your Connection, Fulfillment and Success at Work

Be All You Can Be

Beryl

Editors: Adele Alfano and Kathy Glover Scott ■

Published by

Experts Who Speak Books
www.expertswhospeakbooks.com

ISBN 0-9780283-0-9
©2006 Kathy Glover Scott and Adele Alfano

Editors: Kathy Glover Scott and Adele Alfano
Book design and production: Creative Bound International Inc.
www.creativebound.com

Library and Archives Canada Cataloguing in Publication

Awakening the workplace : achieving connection, fullfillment and success at work / editors: Adele Alfano and Kathy Glover Scott.

ISBN 0-9780283-0-9

1. Quality of work life. 2. Success. I. Alfano, Adele, 1959-
II. Scott, Kathy Glover, 1958- III. Title.
HD6955.A94 2006   650.1   C2006-901559-7

Contents

Introduction

The spark for *Awakening the Workplace* first came to light during our initial planning session for Experts Who Speak Books in 2002. Even at the dawn of our series, as editors we were passionate about sharing the new knowledge and tools needed to address the changes and daily challenges in an ever-evolving workplace. Since that time, we've successfully published six best-selling books with more to come.

With all of the Experts Who Speak Books, our goal is to provide you with tips, tools, motivation and essential information. In *Awakening the Workplace*, you'll find the collective wisdom, experience and knowledge of 16 top speakers, trainers, facilitators, coaches and consultants from across North America and Australia who specialize in workplace issues and innovation. Where else can you find the proven expertise and essential wisdom of 16 top trainers, coaches and consultants in one book? Each have taken the absolute essence of their work and teaching and condensed it into chapter form. And the information in each chapter is written with a focus on providing you with the new tools, skills and systems that you need to excel, all in a format that is easy to read and learn.

What makes *Awakening the Workplace* unique is how it speaks to the reader in a solution-focused way, regardless of their role in whatever size of business or organization—even as a solo entrepreneur. How we execute our workday has rapidly changed and all the old rules for how we should work together have been challenged or thrown out all together. Yet, there are threads of knowledge and expertise that all people who work require. *Awakening the Workplace* reflects the need for this information.

Experts Who Speak Books is one of the most successful book publishing companies in the world specializing in producing books for professional speakers, trainers, facilitators, coaches and consultants. We create co-authored books that showcase the dynamic, creative and successful people who have chosen these professions. We do it through supporting the writing process and taking care of all the specialized work of design, printing, publishing and distribution. And, we do it from a win-win value base, where cost sharing, cross promotion and mutual support are the keys to our success. You are invited to visit our Web sites: www.expertswhospeakbooks.com, www.salesgurusspeakout.com, www.expertwomenspeakout.com and, of course, www.awakeningtheworkplace.com .

Watch for our *Expert Women Who Speak...Speak Out!* Volume 6, as well as upcoming books on subjects that include the Internet, communications, sales and marketing. Let us know if you are in these professions and would like to contribute.

All in all, you are holding in your hands a goldmine of information and expertise, geared to make your work life easier. Our wish is that success flows to you. The choice is yours—to remain where you are or move forward. Not a hard decision to make!

Kathy Glover Scott and Adele Alfano
Editors and Publishers, Experts Who Speak Books

Please visit this book's Web site: www.AwakeningtheWorkplace.com

Paul Huschilt

Tales, Talks, Training, Inc.

An Awake Attitude:
Four Keys That Work at Work

Important news flash: Everyone is falling asleep at work. An Ipsos Reid Survey that aired on CTV in 2002 states that 39 percent of Canadians have trouble falling asleep at night because they are thinking about work. What they don't tell us is that the other 61 percent of Canadians are having trouble staying awake during the day because they are thinking about work. We have a problem here!

If you have a nine-to-five job, arrive on time and don't leave before you are supposed to, then you spend about twice your waking hours at work than you do at home with your loved ones. (This is true, by the way, regardless of how you feel about your loved ones.) The time at work makes up nearly half your conscious adult life. This is a hugely significant piece of the pie. And yet, it seems people everywhere are just snoozing this time away. The following is a case in point:

> There is one word we hear 100,000 times while growing up. Guess what that word is? (the answer later)

>> There was a beloved ex-colleague of mine with whom I gave several good years to the insurance industry—good years that we will never see again. He developed an almost religious practice of sleeping at his desk between the hours of two and three every afternoon. Let's call him Rumplestiltskin.

Early one afternoon, Rumplestiltskin's manager roused him from his sleep, and coaxed him into his office. The dutiful manager inquired at length about Rumplestiltskin's committed approach to sleep. "I am afraid that I cannot allow you to sleep at your desk everyday," informed the manager. "If I let you sleep at your desk, everyone will want to. And since your sleep is so disciplined, you are making us all look bad." **«**

This story certainly supports the argument that the workplace needs to be awakened. Even if it is not exactly true that everybody is falling asleep, we could probably agree that most workplaces could stand to be more fun. According to a survey of managers conducted by the Society of Human Resource Management, almost all respondents felt their workplaces should be more fun for employees. In addition, there was an almost unanimous agreement that fun had no negative effects on the workplace… Let the games begin!

The fact that attitude affects how well a job gets done is a no-brainer. The following little-known tidbit, though, is a good reminder never to let your attitude slip lest you should slip up:

» According to the Merriam-Webster online Dictionary (www.m-w.com), the etymology of the word *attitude* comes from the French, which comes from the Italian, which comes from the Latin *aptitudin* which means *aptitude*. **«**

Learn to master a positive attitude and become a conscious master at what you do. Learn to awaken a work attitude so vital that falling asleep at your desk would be as unconscionable as sleeping through your favorite dessert. Learn to have an attitude so delicious that everyone will want some.

The greatest part of our happiness depends on
our dispositions, not our circumstances.

Martha Washington

The simplest and most reliable way to be happy with our circumstances is to change the way we are with them. The rest of this chapter teaches simple concepts—or keys—that can be hard to put into play. Practice these until they become habit-forming. A positive attitude should not be an act of will. It should happen as naturally as a bad habit that's tough to shake. Then it will come as easily as falling asleep at your desk between two and three every afternoon. Only you will be awake to enjoy the benefits!

Key #1—Manage Your Stress

» An incomplete (and therefore inaccurate) history of stress:

About 400 million years ago (give or take a few days) our ancestors' veins were pumped with adrenalin and stress hormones every time a dinosaur wandered into their backyard. With these stress hormones in their veins, they were able to respond quickly and run like crazy. The fact that you are sitting here today reading this chapter is thanks in part to those stress hormones. You owe them a debt of gratitude.

Flash forward 400 million years (give or take a 40-hour workweek) and you are sitting in your office. Your boss, the lovely person that he is, walks in. Those same stress hormones enter your veins. But this time you don't run. Instead, you sit there and smile. Then, when he leaves, you do what he asked you to. While you are doing it, you worry that you won't get it done and that you will have to stay late. The stress hormones stay with you as long as you think these and other troubling thoughts. As you do, more stress hormones enter your veins. If you build up stress hormones for a long period of time and have no healthy way to release them, those stress hormones (which are the reason you are alive today), could actually kill you. **«**

It is key is to avoid long periods of negative stress because it wreaks havoc on our immune systems. In fact, we now know what we always knew: stress is linked to many diseases the way the White House is linked to the Pentagon by a red phone. Everyone stay calm, but the evidence is pretty high that if we don't find a way to relax soon, somebody is going to get hurt. A positive attitude is impossible without a pulse. Being "up" is easier if you are not "six feet under." The first key to an awake attitude is to manage the stress in your life before it wears you into the ground.

Thankfully, there are things you can do to reduce stress. Many of them are legal. And some of them, you can actually do at your desk.

Adult Education Activity #1

» Right now, take three long, deep breaths. Breathe in all of the fresh air that you can from your workstation, with windows or not, that may or may not open. Then, breathe out all of the frustrations of a lifetime onto the shoulders of the co-workers nearest you. It's as simple as "in with the good air, out with the bad."

Feel the support that is there for you. Feel the support under your feet. Feel the support under your buttocks on the chair. Feel the support at your lower back against the back of the chair. (Notice if this is the closest thing to affection you have felt in years.)

Say hello to your inner self, and use your name. When you do, notice if there is not a wee voice inside that says, "Who are you?" «

That was a bit tongue-in-cheek, but it is really all it takes: just a few moments a day to take a few deep breaths, to feel supported and connected to an inner life. Do this a few times a day for a brighter and cheerier attitude. Research supports that downtime like this has positive health benefits.

Cardiologist Randy Byrd, from San Francisco General Hospital, did a study where he found patients who prayed after a heart attack had fewer complications while in the unit following surgery. Herbert Benson, a Harvard-trained physician, found that transcendental mediation reduced the occurrence of irregular heartbeats present in hypertension.

Even 10 minutes a day will make a difference. My Hatha Yoga teacher, Joy Craighead from the Himalayan Institute of Canada, says that if you do only 10 minutes of yoga a day, you will get the benefit of those 10 minutes. Simple but true. Do you say no to exercise because you do not have enough time? Most of us could squeeze in 10 minutes a day. It is worth it, you deserve it, and it is a good beginning.

If you aren't fired with enthusiasm, you will be fired with enthusiasm.

Vince Lombardi

Key #2—Balance Your Life

Remember the question from the first page? What word do we hear 100,000 times growing up? The answer is "no." Since we hear this word 100,000 times growing up, we learn to have an aversion to it as adults. It is almost impossible for some people to use the word!

"Everything in moderation," said Archimedes, unless of course it was Aristotle. How true even today, because it all comes down to maintaining some kind of balance in life. To do this, you have to learn the Zen-like art of saying no. Say no to things that do not matter and recover time for those that do. Say no to the superfluous and actually have time to floss. If you have moved someone's fridge in the last five years, then you definitely need to learn how to say no.

It comes down to priorities. A university professor of mine, Dr. Richard Florida, (author of *Rise of the Creative Class*, a book about the effect of creativity on economics) introduced the term "to satisfice" in class. (Original source: Herbert Simon's *Models of Man*, 1957.) Here is the definition as I remember it from graduate school:

Satisfice (v) to do the best you can with the limited resources available, including time (from no dictionary at all; not common usage...yet).

Instead of aiming for perfection, do the best you can with what you've got. "Satisfice" and you will not only complete things adequately, you will also find leftover time for you. It is harder to feel a passion for work when worked to the bone. In a complex world, "satisficing" teaches us to do more with less, make quicker decisions, and let go of what's not important.

Because everything we do is limited by space, time and resources, everything we do is a piece of art.

Albert Einstein

Don't worry the next time you feel you don't have what it takes. According to one of the greatest minds in history, you are not about to make a huge mistake, you are about to create a masterpiece.

Key #3—Smile and Laugh More

He who laughs, lasts.

Mary Pettibone Poole

Why don't people smile and laugh more at work? It's simple. They are afraid they will get in trouble. This is because when you laugh, you release chemicals into your bloodstream that would be illegal if you bought them on the street. This is serious stuff.

According to Dr. Lee Berk from Loma Linda University, when you laugh your body releases T-lymphocytes. The penal system would surely lock anyone up who illicitly sold T-lymphocytes to minors outside the gates of school. Thankfully, the eternal wisdom of the universe is such that no one has to. We don't have to push T-lymphocytes because laughter itself is contagious. When you laugh, not only do you benefit from these immunity building chemicals, those who can't help but laugh with you also benefit.

During those years in insurance when I had a terrible attitude, there were days when I reported to work simply to hear the woman in the next cubicle laugh. Her laugh was as contagious as the common cold, only you wanted to get it. I used to lean against the synthetic beige fabric of the cubicle partition that separated her professional world from mine, hoping to catch whatever it was that she had. She did not laugh at anything particularly funny. She just laughed. And every time she did, I felt closer to her, closer to life, closer to insurance. Her joyful laughter made me feel the truth in the title words of the Walt Disney song "It's a Small World After All."

The shortest distance between two people is laughter.

Victor Borge

In 1987, Dr. Kathleen Dillon and others found that when you laugh, the body releases salivary immunoglobulin-A. It sounds as gross as scary vegetables you've never tried, but this is actually good for you. Immunoglobulin-A is the body's first defense against invading micro-organisms.

Not only that, there are physiological benefits, as well. The poker face that seems to be standard issue in the workplace gets tugged and squeezed in all sorts of clownish ways. This releases tension and increases circulation. With more blood flowing, you get more oxygen. With more oxygen, you feel better and can think more clearly. Not to mention the proven fact that those who breathe oxygen regularly actually live longer!

It is a commonly held belief that if you have too much fun at work, you won't get your work done. In the extreme that might be true. But somewhere between swinging from the fluorescents and boring oneself to death by sitting on one's own spirit, there has to be workable middle ground.

Laughing and smiling more at work will lighten your attitude, make you professionally irresistible to co-workers, and fill you with enthusiasm. Laugh more with others and you will spread this socially acceptable spasm and infect those you work with and/or love with joy. Find time to laugh with colleagues and turn your workplace into a jungle gym of chemically induced camaraderie. Share embarrassing stories from your own life (always a good source of humor). Collect and post funny cartoons. Slip into a clown nose whenever you feel yourself getting stressed. Keep a rubber chicken next to the stapler. Play simple games at lunch and on breaks that get you and your co-workers having fun together.

How welcome a little more laughter would be in the workplace (if only to wake some people up). Laughter is not an over-the-counter solution to all workplace ills. It will not wipe away the hard stuff, but it will help to keep things in perspective. Although we all know that work has to get done, we could probably all use the occasional reminder that, beyond that, it is just not that serious.

Key #4—Clean Your Inner Closet

*You cannot do anything great in this world. You can only
do small things with great love.*

Mother Teresa

At the age of 27, I took a job with computers that I loved to hate. The day-to-day stress of that hatred really got me down. But I was committed to hating work and I was too proud to stop until I had developed the perfect negative attitude toward a job

I felt was too small for me. Five years into that job, I developed the repetitive strain injury called carpal tunnel syndrome. The condition was so bad that it was impossible to sleep at night. It seemed there were two choices: either do something for myself, or have surgery. Not one for the scalpel, I chose to do something for myself.

The process I turned to is called "Focusing." To "Focus," you listen to a sense of something inside your body that is vague, unclear and connected to your life. This sense that you pay attention to in Focusing is called the "Felt Sense" because it is more than a feeling and is bodily felt. If you allow the Felt Sense to be exactly as it is, it comes more into focus (hence the name Focusing). Focusing was discovered by Eugene T. Gendlin, Ph.D. from the University of Chicago. He wrote about it in his best-selling book *Focusing* (Bantam Books, 1978).

The last section of this chapter tells the story of how this simple but powerful process called Focusing can change attitudes in positive and surprising ways.

One morning I sat quietly contemplating the dilemma I was in. In a nutshell, the pain from the carpal tunnel seemed to make it impossible to continue at the job I hated, and I could not imagine finding the energy to do something more appealing.

I sat quietly and listened inwardly with unconditional positive regard to how the body experienced the problem. Of course, the first thing I noticed was the pain in the wrists. But as I did, allowing them to feel their pain fully, I was surprised by an intense and uncomfortable knot in the gut. "What does this knot in my gut have to do with the problem in my wrists?" I wondered.

The knot in the gut seemed to need my attention even more than the wrists did, so I stayed with it. As I did, the knot eased a little and I could feel how it contained many negative emotions around work, such as anger, disappointment and worry.

At this point, it was very important to not try to fix the problem or make it better. The key was to let it be exactly how it was.

As I listened acceptingly to the knot in the gut, the knot itself began to find ways of reconnecting with other parts that could offer support. It felt more connected to the shoulders, the legs, the arms, and even the wrists. This sense of integration was accompanied by a subtle inner-directed movement. The movement did not make sense to me, but I allowed it because it seemed to know what I needed. To finish up, I spent a few moments feeling grateful for the insights, feelings and movement that were a part of the process. Then, I forgot about it and went to work.

It is ironic that as soon as I accept myself as I am, then I can change.

Carl Rogers

When I sat at the computer that day, I was shocked to discover that the pain that had been a part of my life for years was gone. The tension that was chronically there at work was replaced by a relaxed and integrated way of key stroking. Miraculously, it was actually pleasurable to sit and do the job I had hated.

What's more, I no longer felt hatred for my job. In fact, it was just the opposite. The word to best describe how I felt about work at that moment was "love." That sense of love became the guiding force in a vital new attitude at work. Work was never the same. Instead of wishing I was doing something more important, I learned to love the little job I was doing and to provide the best service I could with all the love I could muster.

Using this approach daily helped maintain this attitude. Whenever I felt pulled into negative emotions on the job, I allowed them to be as they were and drew on the feeling of love instead. The negative emotions inevitably transformed into a caring attitude that I chose repeatedly to bring to work.

Focusing is a natural process that we all do. When we learn to do it consciously, it holds tremendous promise. The power of listening to how the body experiences life situations without argument, without fixing or judging makes deep-rooted positive change possible.

Adult Education Activity #2:

» Through this exercise, you will experience a simple Focusing process. To do this, imagine someone you know who makes you feel really good about yourself. This could be a real person, or it could be a fictitious hero that you admire.

Once you have that person in mind, think of several words that describe how they make you feel.

Now, take a few moments and imagine yourself in their presence. Invite a bodily Felt Sense of how it feels to be with them. Listen inwardly in the center of your body as that sense begins to form. As the Felt Sense forms, notice how it is more holistic than words we think of mentally.

With your awareness on the Felt Sense, notice what word or phrase or image seems to describe it. When something presents itself, check with the Felt Sense. See if it is a good fit or not. When it is, the Felt Sense often shifts or releases a bit. When it is not, you will know because it won't feel quite right.

Allow the Felt Sense to be exactly as it is. As you do, you might begin to notice the many aspects of it. This is a time when you can even ask it questions. You might ask it, for example, "What is it about this that is so [*insert the word that came to describe your Felt Sense*]?" or, "What is the best of this?" When you ask questions, listen to the Felt Sense and notice how it responds.

Take a few more moments to sit with this, and then wind down the process. Be sure to acknowledge all that has come with gratitude. Know that you can revisit this Focusing place if you wish. Gently bring your awareness back to your surroundings. If you feel like it, make note of what took place. **«**

Focusing is a gentle yet powerful tool for positive change. The act of listening inwardly without judgment to how the body experiences life issues frees up energy to be your best. Focusing is great for decision making, for removing blocks to action, even for working through perceived conflict. It is a powerful problem-solving tool that works equally well with creative projects and unleashing peak performance.

The World's Shortest Focusing Lesson

Focusing takes place with an unconditional positive regard called the Focusing Attitude. The following are some elements to assist you in learning this powerful technique:

Find a Felt Sense: Do what you need to do to get more centered as you gradually bring your awareness into your body. Ask yourself, "What do I want to Focus on right now?" With your awareness inside, allow a Felt Sense of that issue to form.

Get a Handle: With your awareness on the Felt Sense, ask yourself what word, phrase or image describes how it is right now.

Resonate: When a word, phrase or image emerges, check it with the Felt Sense to see if it fits. Repeat this several times and notice how the Felt Sense shifts and reveals more.

Ask: Ask questions of the Felt Sense, such as, "What is the worst of this?" "What is the best of this?" "What is the new edge here?" "What does this want me to know right now?"

Receive: After listening to the Felt Sense for a while, you will likely come to a place that feels like a natural ending spot. Acknowledge what came with a sense of gratitude. Know that you can choose to return to this anytime. Bring your awareness back to the room.

Paul acknowledges the Focusing Institute for their encouragement and written approval for writing about Dr. Eugene T. Gendlin's work called Focusing.

For more information about Focusing, visit the Focusing Institute at www.focusing.org. The site lists many resources, including certified teachers by region, books and courses.

Wrapping It All Up

Well, gentle reader, are you still awake? It's been fun, but before you get too weary, it is time to move on to another chapter. Bravely continue on your personal path to wakefulness. As you go, remember to find time to relax, keep things in perspective, laugh lots, and live life from the inside out. You might want to set aside some time periodically to plan ahead. Ask yourself what you need to do if things ever got so harried that you might otherwise forget to take good care. Develop a plan so you will always remember to reserve time for yourself and to smile and laugh your way through whatever work has to offer. Most of all, accept yourself as you are to set in motion a powerful movement toward personal growth and a "great attitude"— or for short, "gratitude."

Paul Huschilt

Award-winning professional speaker and storyteller **Paul Huschilt** is one of the most unique talents in the speaking industry. Paul converts what happens at conferences into on-the-spot musical spoofs. His conference closings are one-of-a-kind and completely focused on the client. Other programs include Seven Humor Habits for Workplace Wellness, Everybody Stay Calm, and The Fool Climbs It Twice. Happy clients include the CIBC, RBC Financial Group, Janssen-Ortho Inc., FedEx, Whirlpool Canada, The Canadian Museums Association, Queens University, Ryerson University, Sheridan College, Canadian Heritage, Canada Council for the Arts, Health Canada and all levels of government.

Paul is best known for creating corporate community through storytelling and by re-awakening peoples' passion for what they love to do most in a riotously funny manner. He is an emerging expert in the area of humor and workplace wellness and a published author of the interactive desk calendar *Seven Humor Habits for Workplace Wellness*. He is the recipient of the 2003 Association for Psychological Type Award for Innovation in Education and Training, the 2004 Brian Lee Mastery in Performance Award and the 2005 Hamilton Niagara Chapter of CAPS, "Member of the Year" award.

Business Name:	Tales, Talks, Training, Inc.
Address:	15 Dermott Place, Toronto, ON M5A 3B5
Telephone:	416-324-2730
Fax:	416-324-2733
E-mail:	paul@paulhuschilt.com
Web Address:	www.paulhuschilt.com
Professional Affiliations:	Professional member, Canadian Association of Professional Speakers and National Speakers Association

Crystal Flaman

Tandem Communications

Focused Action = Exponential Results

Are you ready to live the *best year* of your life on both a professional and personal level? Imagine if you could have your best year ever, starting *today*! What would this year look like for you? Can you visualize living every day more fulfilled and energized than ever before, where your life has immeasurable purpose? Can you see yourself deriving more satisfaction from your work, surpassing last year's revenue targets and profits? Or, perhaps the best year of your life would be a year where "it all falls into place" and you find you are achieving more with less effort expended and you are able to juggle all aspects of your work and personal life! How does that sound to you? All of these things are available to you when you are ready to welcome them into your life.

What would the catalyst need to be for you to actually live the best year of your life? What would you have to do differently in order to attract motivated and positive people, who share in your goals? Think about this for a moment. What would actually need to happen or take place in the world?

- A new boss or different co-workers?
- An economic boom or a change in the interest rates?
- A change in your physical location or expansion into new markets?
- Winning a lottery or having your bills magically erased?
- Losing 20 pounds or meeting that special someone?

Or, perhaps, rather than require one or more of these external events, as a catalyst to create the best year of your life, you simply need to look in the mirror for the answer. Imagine the possibilities and potential results! A few small changes, made every day, stacked on top of one another, combined together to attract and create the most incredible, fabulous and fulfilling year you've ever imagined! Imagine if you lived by the motto: **Become more than you were when you woke up this morning!**

It *is* possible to create your most successful professional and personal year of your life by simply waking up and doing a few small but significant things every day. These specific things, when added together, have exponential value and power to launch you into an entirely new world of fulfillment and success. A place in life so powerful and filled with opportunities that few rarely even dream of it!

Awakening the workplace is about awakening YOU! It's about waking up the spirit and energy inside of you and sharing your talents and gifts with those around you, at work and elsewhere. This includes your colleagues, staff, supervisors, customers…in fact, absolutely everyone you come into contact with at the office and at home. It's about waking up with a sense of purpose and living that purpose on a daily basis, regardless of your affinity for your job or business. You may be very happy with what you've achieved and are content and comfortable. Some of you, on the other hand, may be extremely frustrated, suffocated and stifled in your environment, filled with an overwhelming sense of emptiness. Regardless of your current satisfaction, or lack of it, know that you are not defined by your job or your business. Over the next few pages, you'll discover ways to enhance not only your work, but also the life you are living! You will start to live the best year of your life, filled with passion, joy and fulfillment. The way to do this is by simply making a few small yet significant changes, every day, in a specific direction towards your greater purpose!

Let's get started with four action steps to awakening the workplace and living your best year now!

Action Step #1—Evaluate the Present

Are you ready for the best year of your life? This may seem like a ridiculous question, but let's see if you are indeed ready for it. To start, you need to be ready to honestly assess where you are now and how you've chosen to live your life:

- Are you ready to let go of baggage from the past?
- Are you open to shifting your thinking and reducing negative thoughts or experiences, false judgments and grudges?
- Are you ready to let go of false beliefs about yourself and others and be open to living life in a more fulfilling way?

Look over your shoulder and assess the baggage you are carrying. It is what follows you like a shadow. Let it go. You don't need it any longer. If you're swimming in a rut that feels so deep that you can't get out, be assured and just believe that with the help of the tips on the next few pages, you'll find your way, by simply doing a few things differently every day.

What Does Your Current Status Look Like?

The following tool will help you to evaluate the present. Take some time to assess and critique your current situation on a personal and professional/business level. Objectively assess and rate yourself in each of the following areas of your life on a scale from 1 to 10, with 1 being very dissatisfied and 10 being extremely satisfied. Write your rating (between 1 and 10) beside the corresponding measure. Be honest and objective. Evaluate your present life as if you are on the outside looking in.

Personal

Overall physical health		Overall emotional health		Overall appearance		Take time for hobbies	
Balanced life		Weight		Laugh often		Fitness level	
Feel valued as a person by family and friends		Spend quality time with family and friends		Trusts and listens to intuition		Take time to relax, have fun and dream	

Have close friends to talk to and have fun with		Satisfied with personal savings, net worth, investments		Satisfied with level of spiritual connection and growth		Happy and secure with relationship with partner or spouse		
Freedom to make decisions		Enough sleep		Organized home		Have a sense of personal purpose		

Total rating: _____/200

Professional/Business

Feel appreciated and valued at work		Eager to get up and get to work in the morning		Hopeful about future with organization		Ability to control many aspects of work		
Remuneration or pay is adequate		Overall satisfaction with work life		Feel able to get ahead of workload		Give adequate time to clients		
Able to meet customers' needs most of the time		Able to learn, expand skills and continually grow at work		Surrounded by positive, supportive people		Room for advancement and growth		
Positive outlook for future financial prosperity		Positive and professional business image and reputation		Feel confident and empowered at work		Enthusiasm for day-to-day activities at work		
Organized office/work space		Empowered to make decisions at work		Able to use creativity and imagination		Have fun at work		

Total rating: _____/200

Now, for both sections, add up your ratings (between 1 and 10). The following is the rating scale for each area:

Above 160 for each section: Extremely satisfied. You are extremely satisfied with your life and everything in it! You are surrounded by supportive, positive people and are appreciated. You have designed your life in a way that works for you and you have a great sense of freedom and opportunity. Congratulations!

Between 110 and 160: Satisfied. There are certain areas of your life that you would like to change, but you are satisfied with most aspects. Take a look at the areas where you rated yourself 6 or lower and try to make just a few changes in order to become more satisfied in these areas. Congratulations on the areas in which you rated yourself 8 or higher! Many aspects of your life are working very well.

Between 90 and 110: Slightly dissatisfied. There are many aspects of your life that work well for you, but there are a number of key areas in which you are not satisfied. Clearly, you are experiencing some sense of frustration or disappointment with your work and/or personal life. Choose one or two areas you rated at less than 5 and think about possible actions you could take to increase satisfaction in these areas. Focus on one area at a time, not everything at once.

Below 100: Extremely dissatisfied. Currently, you are experiencing a great deal of dissatisfaction with your work and/or personal life. There may be many reasons for this that you cannot control. Now is the time to put yourself first in your life and focus on your needs and wants. The more you can rejuvenate yourself right now, the more productive and successful you will be at work. Focus on just one area and think of how you can increase your joy and satisfaction in that area.

Action Step #2—Create the Picture

Many years ago, while enrolled in a course entitled Human Relations 201, my professor, Dan Sydiah, asked each student to write down their short-term and long-term goals. He cited the example of a study following up the Yale University class of 1953:

> » In 1953, Yale University surveyed its graduating class and discovered
> that only 3 percent had written goals. Twenty years later, Yale surveyed
> this same class and learned that the 3 percent who had written goals had

accumulated a net worth or wealth greater than the other 97 percent combined. **«**

Considering this example and with enthusiasm for the possible long-term results, I wrote down a long list of goals and dreams. I dreamed of my ideal life: being surrounded by happy, positive people, owning my own business, taking several months off each year to travel the globe, to name just a few of my goals. In just four years, I found myself living my dreams! I had just spent a month traveling in Brazil and was driving to one of my businesses (a hostel for international travelers), sipping on a coffee, enjoying the early morning sunshine that being awake at 6:30 am offers, and I was surrounded by international travelers—by nature are incredibly positive people—and enjoying the rewards and freedom of owning two successful businesses.

Over the years, other goals were written down and accomplished. These included skydiving, competing in an Ironman triathlon, owning several lucrative real estate properties, cycling across Canada and running a 100-kilometer race in the process of helping others. My twin sister, Carla, also had a desire to help others, and together, we cycled on the first-ever tandem bicycle to cross Canada in 1994, raising thousands of dollars for charity. In December 2005, my colleague Stephanie Moore and I ran 100 kilometers, in support of a local charity, Partners in the Horn of Africa. I know from first-hand experience that committing your goals to paper is the key to turning your dreams into reality!

Determining Your Goals

The first step is to discover what the best year of your life would look like for you! We don't get what we want in life, we get what we picture! In fact, our brain functions in pictures. We actually "think" in pictures, and these pictures are then translated into thoughts, dreams and words. So, take some time to vividly *picture* what you would like to see included in your life. Close your eyes and imagine. The key is to be specific, to dream big and to really be bold in this process!

Take out a blank sheet of paper (the larger the better). The purpose of this exercise is to commit to paper, the dreams and goals you have inside your mind.

Because, once you allow them to escape beyond the boundaries of your mind, onto paper, they begin to take shape and manifest in reality.

Focus on the best and allow it to manifest!

You may wish to write down, in words, all the things that would be included in the best year of your life. Or, you may wish to actually cut pictures out of magazines. Choose whichever method works best for you, and dream on paper what you see in your ideal year. The following are some topic areas you may wish to include:

- Career, work, business success, rewards;
- Financial, investments, savings, net worth;
- Personal health, fitness, weight, appearance and grooming;
- Home or residence, environment, geographical location;
- New purchases, such as a car, bike, furniture or flat-screen plasma TV;
- Friendships, relationships, family, children;
- Spirituality;
- Holidays, time off, freedom, travel, hobbies, sports, interests, adventures, passion;
- New learning.

To achieve these goals, it helps to break them down into small steps or chunks. Emulate one of those 3 percent in 1953! Write down your goals and dreams and reap the rewards that are out there, almost waiting for you. Be specific in your picture and write down all that you would like to see take shape in the next year of your life, even if you're not sure how they might materialize. Have fun! Think big! Be bold and dream big dreams!

Action Step #3—Discover Your Purpose

What is your purpose? What legacy would you like to leave behind you? What talents can you share at home, in your work and in your community? How are you currently utilizing your gifts and living your purpose?

Purpose can be defined as your calling or mission in life. When people live with a sense of purpose, their life takes on greater meaning, direction and power! Examples of individuals who have lived with an insatiable purpose include Mother Theresa, Oprah, Martin Luther King, Wayne Gretzky and Lance Armstrong. These people were or are driven by their own personal sense of purpose in life and have left an undeniable legacy and contribution to the world. I heard long ago that "when the why becomes large enough, the how becomes easy." This means that if the reason we want something becomes so vivid and clear, how we achieve it or obtain it becomes easy.

Take a moment to think of your own sense of purpose. Think about your passion, what inspires and motivates you, and what sort of contribution you are making in the world. Focus on your gifts. Your passion. Your talents and skills. Spend some time considering the amazing strengths you possess! Write them down.

Looking at your list, do you see where you are currently sharing your passion and talents in your work life? Consider the areas of your work and personal life that you are very satisfied with. It is in these areas that your energy and efforts can be transformed into the contribution you are making in your world. Can you see where you could awaken your inner purpose and incorporate your passion, talents, skills and gifts even more at work? Awakening the workplace is truly about awakening you and living your own personal higher purpose every day, to create greater joy and satisfaction in your own life and the lives of those around you!

Action Step #4—Focus on Today

By focusing on today, you will have exponential results in all your tomorrows. The following are seven simple yet powerful things you can do *today* to awaken your workplace, positively influence your colleagues and create the best year of your life NOW! Watch what happens, when your efforts take effect, day after day, creating exponential value.

1. Commit to becoming the most positive person you know. Attitude is a choice! Choose your attitude every day, at work and at home. Use visual reminders in your office, your car or at home to help keep your attitude in check. Your perception is your reality, so make it your reality to become the most positive person you know. Refuse to allow negative thoughts or words to enter your mind or leave your mouth. You will discover that your workplace will become a very different place with this one simple shift in your thinking. The results will leave you speechless!

2. Discover what truly motivates you. Discover what stimulus has the ability to instantly influence your behavior, performance and mood. As Thomas Edison said, "If we did all the things we are capable of doing, we would literally astonish ourselves." Discover what motivates you at work and empowers you to be more productive and inspired. At home, do the same things, whether it's music, exercise, nature, a walk in the sun, looking at photos of your family or meditating. Think about how productive you are in the few days prior to leaving on a holiday, and find ways to ignite this energy and motivation to perform at this level on a daily basis. If you are unsure of what motivates you, try to imagine moments when, for some reason, you instantly felt great or when you instantly had a burst of energy. Dissect these moments and find out what prompted these changes. We have the power to instantly change the mood we're in, the state of our mind and the energy levels of our bodies, and we can tap into it at any time by understanding ourselves better and taking advantage of these stimuli!

3. Commit to creating optimum physical health within your body. Start small! Assessing your physical health and doing just one thing every day towards improving your physical health will bring you closer to living the best year of your life. In your workplace, initiate some sort of wellness or health program, considering that health is vital to all and so often neglected.

4. Be grateful for the many things in your work and home life. Look at your current life and take account of the numerous things you are grateful for. Make a list of all the things you can think of. Review it every day, and every day find one more thing to be thankful for and add it to the list. In addition, think back through your life and make a list of all the people who helped you on some level, all the people you are thankful for or who made a difference in your life, who added value to it. This list could contain 20, 30 or 100 names. Each Monday morning, get in touch with one or two of these individuals via e-mail, phone or mail, and express your thanks. Tell them why you are thankful for their presence in your life. You will invariably need 10 to 20 minutes for this exercise, and the rewards will be invaluable. What a way to start the week! Each Monday morning, do the same thing at work and express your gratitude to someone for their contribution to the workplace.

5. Commit to your priorities! Make a list of the three most important tasks you need to do at work tomorrow. Then, tomorrow, when you get to work, do these three things first *before you do anything else*. This suggestion has been used by countless individuals and is responsible for the accumulation of great wealth and prosperity for these individuals. Mary Kay Ash (of Mary Kay Cosmetics) incorporated this suggestion and it had a phenomenal influence on her success. The exponential value of this exercise alone, repeated over time, will single-handedly launch you into living a rewarding, fulfilling life!

6. Document your goals. Commit to writing down your goals on paper. Revisit them often and continually monitor your progress. If you consistently set goals for yourself, you are probably experiencing tremendous results. If you do not currently set goals for yourself, consider the price you are paying (in lost revenue, lost satisfaction, lost time and more) and realize the amount of regret you will have to live with in the future. Set even small goals and discipline yourself to achieve them. Then move on to larger goals and dreams.

7. Find some way to contribute to the world through your work. As Jim Rohn once said, "The key to greatness is to find a way to serve or help others." Find a reason—a purpose—and make a difference in this area. This can be as simple as volunteering to initiate a recycling program or "clothing for the homeless" program in your office. Imagine the personal satisfaction you and your co-workers would gain! Our lives become more fulfilled with each moment we choose to contribute to the betterment of our workplace and world around us.

Showcase your talents and skills! Share your gifts and live your purpose by reviewing these four action steps regularly to keep you on track, and by taking focused action every day:

- Take some time to **evaluate your current situation** and look for significant areas that you are both satisfied and dissatisfied with!
- **Create a dynamic picture** for your ideal work and home life!
- **Discover your purpose** and the incredible gifts that you possess and offer at work! Use opportunities that you have available to you, to allow your purpose to be expressed on a regular basis.
- **Focus, every day,** on the things you can control and influence at work and in your life, including maintaining a positive attitude, creating optimum health, developing an attitude of gratitude, goal-setting and contribution to the world around you.

Awaken the spirit in YOU and live the best year of your life starting NOW! What are you waiting for?

Crystal Flaman

Crystal Flaman is a dynamic facilitator, keynote speaker, entrepreneur, three-time Ironman Triathlete and 100-kilometer ultramarathoner! She combines her positive, energetic and dynamic personality with her success as an entrepreneur and experience in business to inspire people to achieve their dreams, goals and potential.

Crystal has raised hundreds of thousands of dollars for charities, including the Heart and Stroke Foundation and Partners in The Horn of Africa through her athletic pursuits. With her twin sister, Carla Flaman, Crystal cycled across Canada on the first-ever tandem bike to cross the country in support of HSFC and is recognized in the *Guinness Book Of World Records* for this accomplishment. Crystal ran a 100-kilometer ultra-marathon with colleague Stephanie Moore, raising funds for Partners in the Horn of Africa. The money raised from this event supported over 100 women in starting their own micro-businesses in Ethiopia! Crystal consistently pushes the boundaries of what's possible by believing that *anything* can be accomplished and each of us can make an incredible difference in the world by sharing our own unique gifts and talents.

Crystal has been invited as a motivational keynote speaker and facilitator to work with countless large and small businesses, groups and organizations, where her inspiration and humor complement her proven message that our goals and dreams are within our grasp if we have focus, vision and passion! Topics include: Marketing, Sales, Motivation, Communication Skills, Networking, Goal-setting, Achieving Your Dreams, Overcoming Obstacles and Customer Service. Crystal also works with aspiring entrepreneurs to help them turn their dreams into reality.

Business Name: Tandem Communications
Address: Box 121 Station PBC, Kelowna, BC V1Y 7N5
Telephone: 250-215-2903
E-mail: info@crystalflaman.com
Web Address: www.crystalflaman.com
Professional Affiliations: Canadian Association of Professional Speakers

Sandra Greenough, CHRP

Greenough & Associates Inc.

Spiritual Passion in Your Workplace and Life

It is with the heart that one sees rightly; what is essential is invisible to the eye.

Antoine de Saint-Exupery

We hear about "Spiritual Passion" increasingly today, yet what does this really mean? Being spiritual is the connection to the spirit through relationships with people, sacred objects, rituals and places. It concerns the spirit or higher moral qualities, and is often thought of with regard to religion. Spirituality is the personal growth of one's true self through spiritual connections. Spiritual Passion is the dynamic force enabling you to live your life and soul's purpose through the connection of your intellectual, emotional, spiritual and physical being.

Father Tredget, a Benedictine monk, notes that the word spirituality derives from the Latin verb *spirare*, to breathe, and the noun *spiritus*, a breath, so it involves ideas of energy or a force behind life. He also says, "When you read the world's literature on spirituality, there are some common themes that emerge. That Spirituality involves growth—about becoming a person in the fullest sense. It involves relationships, perhaps a kind of spiritual hospitality towards others. It embraces a person's intellect, emotions and their soul and it animates a person's attitudes, beliefs, behavior and practices."

The Importance of Spiritual Passion

You are not alone in your search for a spiritually centered workplace and life. The thirst and hunger for understanding and connecting with your spirituality has been a quest since the beginning of time and is as essential as the food you eat to your happiness, health, productivity, relationships and well-being.

Spiritual Passion enables you to "chart the unknown" and climb the mountains of life with courage, determination, focus and humility. Spiritual Passion connects you with a thankful heart and the ability to enjoy a culture of abundance...to genuinely celebrate the success of others rather than being threatened by it.

Writing in *The European Business Review* in 2005, Corinne McLauglin noted: "People at all levels in the corporate hierarchy increasingly want to nourish their spirit and creativity. When employees are encouraged to express their creativity, the result is a more fulfilled and sustained workforce. Happy people work harder and are more likely to stay at their jobs. A study of business performance by the highly respected Wilson Learning Company found that 39 percent of the variability in corporate performance is attributable to the personal satisfaction of the staff. Spirituality was cited as the second most important factor in personal happiness (after health) by the majority of Americans questioned in a *USA Weekend* poll, with 47 percent saying that spirituality was the most important element of their happiness."

McLaughlin continued, "The spirituality in business movement is one of the hopeful signs that business, as the most powerful institution in the world today, may be transforming from within. What is emerging is a new attitude towards the workplace as a place to fulfill one's deeper purpose. As World Business Academy co-founder Willis Harman remarked, 'The dominant institution in any society needs to take responsibility for the whole, as the church did in the days of the Holy Roman Empire.'"

Each day, more and more business people are helping to create a better world by being more socially responsible in how they treat people and the environment. They are proving that spirituality helps, rather than harms, the bottom line.

Work is love made visible.
Kahlil Gibran, *The Prophet*

In exploring spirituality at work here, you will be guided through my original Spiritual Passion Sort, an assessment tool and planning process to assist you in applying your insights to strengthen your spirituality This chapter also provides inspirational and strategically practical insights and tips from the lessons of others to help you strengthen your spiritual confidence and connections in your workplace and life.

Your Spiritual Passion

Earlier, I defined Spiritual Passion as the dynamic force enabling you to live your life and soul's purpose through the connection of your intellectual, emotional, physical and spiritual being. Spiritual Passion enables you to work and live in harmony with your inner core values, beliefs and priorities.

An example of how you can connect with your dynamic spiritual force in the workplace is when you are highly motivated to take on challenges, identify needs and develop solutions you believe will address an injustice, inequality or priority in your workplace, economy, family or community.

Another example is when you coach and guide others to achieve their full potential in the workplace, when you volunteer on behalf of your organization to strengthen the community, when you show kindness and when you inspire others through supportive words and actions. The following questions will help you focus on your perspective. Record your answers on a blank piece of paper.

- How do you see Spiritual Passion in action by others at work?
- How do you express Spiritual Passion in your workplace?

Spiritual Passion Self-Assessment Tool

Now I would like to guide you through a Spiritual Passion self-assessment tool. It is designed to help you identify areas in your work and life that can:

- Help you develop and strengthen your connection with your Spiritual Passion;
- Cause you Spiritual Pain and Spiritual Void (a feeling of emptiness for you). These will be areas that diminish your Spirit, break your Spirit, drain your energies and zest for work and life;

- Heal and strengthen you to move from Spiritual Pain and Void to Spiritual Development and Strength;
- Assist you to focus your Spiritual Passion Plan and include positive action steps to strengthen your spiritual connection.

Please take a deep breath, relax and enjoy the process. If you feel uncomfortable, please remember that is nature's way of telling you that you are stretching, growing and learning…similar to when you were a child and had growing pains.

Spiritual Passion Sort Instructions

Please complete this assessment when you are well-rested and uninterrupted. Prepare your mind, emotions, spirit and body for this process. You may wish to enjoy a walk, meditate, listen to music or have a warm bath to help you reach a relaxed state before beginning. Do create an environment, space and time that will be conducive to honest, personal reflection. Use a blank piece of paper for recording your responses to each question.

When you reflect on each question, think of all areas of your work, life and volunteer activities. There is no right or wrong response, only your personal truth. Please be honest with yourself, as this will give you powerful and useful information for your plan.

Spiritual Passion Sort

Step 1: Spiritual Strength

These are your knowledge, skills, attitudes and behaviors that connect with your purpose and intention in work and life. These are your powerful sources of strength, energy, confidence, courage and action.

Examples of Spiritual Strength in your workplace and life:

- Smiling and providing positive, constructive feedback
- Communicating to people with respect
- Offering to assist your colleagues
- Providing enthusiastic customer service
- Taking a self-directed approach to work, career and life

- Connecting with positive, spiritually centered people
- Working with dedicated professionals of integrity
- Enjoying nature, music and art
- Praying and/or meditating
- Regular physical and recreational activity
- Volunteering on behalf of your organization or yourself

My Spiritual Strength

- What are the greatest sources of your Spiritual Strength? Include some sources from your workplace.

Spiritual Strength Review

Please take a look at and feel the positive connection you have with your spirituality through your work and life activities. Congratulations on recognizing what is working well in your work and life's activities!

Later on when you develop your Spiritual Passion Plan, please remember to stay connected with these strengthening activities.

Step 2: Spiritual Pain

Spiritual Pain is when you hold yourself back or are not allowed to connect with your spirituality. These are areas for healing and strengthening to help you move from Spiritual Pain to Spiritual Strength and Joy.

Examples of Spiritual Pain in your workplace and life:

- Communication or behavior that is discriminatory, dishonest, disrespectful, negative, toxic, violent, destructive or passive aggressive
- Low self-confidence regarding your work and personal performance
- Excessive workloads that put pressure on your ability to live a balanced life
- Loss of a close co-worker, relative or friend
- Constant waves of change and turbulence in the workplace
- Unhealthy relationships that erode your self-esteem and break your spirit
- Financial pressures

My Spiritual Pain

Identifying areas of Spiritual Pain is one of the most important ways you can begin to turn your pain into strength and fuel. You need to be aware of what is causing you pain so you can develop an action plan.

- What is causing me Spiritual Pain in my work and life?

Spiritual Pain Review

Now that you have identified aspects of your work and life that are causing you Spiritual Pain, ask yourself these questions:

- Percentage-wise, how much of my work and life is causing me Spiritual Pain and how is this pain affecting my work and life?
- Am I prepared to continue working and living with this much Spiritual Pain? If so, why?
- What will be the cost to my work performance, personal and volunteer happiness if I continue to live with this Spiritual Pain?
- With whom can I confidentially discuss these concerns and who will help me identify action steps to move away from Spiritual Pain to Spiritual Strength?

When you develop your Spiritual Passion Plan, you will have the opportunity to set goals and identify action steps to turn your pain into healing and Spiritual Strength.

Step 3: Spiritual Void (a feeling of emptiness)

These are areas in your work and life that break your spirit, drain your energies and zest for work and life that not only cause you pain, but are a real area of emptiness for you.

Examples of Spiritual Void in your workplace and life:

- Dishonest or disrespectful communication and/or behaviors
- Toxic, unhealthy comments from co-workers, family, friends, volunteers that erode your self-esteem or the self-esteem of others
- Conflict without constructive positive resolution
- Unethical and destructive "political" agendas
- Egotistical, self-centered behaviors
- Not feeling connected with work and life purpose

- Dissatisfaction and feeling something is deeply missing in your work or life
- Severe loneliness or sadness
- Feeling trapped, in a deep rut and seeing no way out
- Being afraid of the unknown and the future
- Stark working environment, limited natural lighting, lack of opportunity to take breaks

My Spiritual Void
- What is creating a Spiritual Void in your work and life?

Spiritual Void Review

Now examine the areas of your work and life that are breaking and diminishing your spirit, draining your energies and zest for life. Ask yourself these questions:

- How much of my work and life is creating a Spiritual Void and how is it affecting my work and life?
- Am I prepared to continue working and living with this Spiritual Void? If so, why?
- What will be the cost to my work performance, personal and volunteer happiness if I continue to live with this Spiritual Void?
- With whom can I confidentially discuss these concerns and who will help me identify action steps to move away from a Spiritual Void to Spiritual Development and Strength?

When you develop your Spiritual Passion Plan, you will have the opportunity to set goals and identify action steps to turn your void into healing and Spiritual Strength.

Step 4: Spiritual Development

This is your area for strengthening your connection with your purpose in work and life, energy, confidence, courage, action and joy.

Examples of ways to develop spiritually:

- Assess which areas of my work aligns with who I really am
- Find a coach and/or mentor for myself
- Continue to personally and professionally learn and develop

- Enjoy time in nature
- Take better care of my health and well-being
- Take up recreational activities that inspire creativity
- Connect with more spiritually centered people
- Connect with people from different spiritual perspectives

Spiritual Development Review

What are my top three development priorities over the next year? Ask yourself: how and when can I develop these three priority development areas?

Spiritual Passion Plan

Now is your opportunity to develop a Spiritual Passion Plan to help you maintain and strengthen your Spiritual Passion connection with your work, life and volunteer service.

Think about the long-term and short-term goals upon which you need to focus. When forming goals, be focused on the time frame you set and the resources that you will need to accomplish them. Using a clean piece of paper, write down the following headings:

Overall Goal

Long-term goal # 1   Start date: End date:

Resources required (these can be people, time, things or environments)**:**

Short-term goal #1   Start date: End date:

Resources required (these can be people, time, things or environments)**:**

List the next ones as Short-term goal #2 and Long-term goal #2. Repeat this for as many short-term and long-term goals you have as part of your overall goal.

Here is an example of what your Spiritual Passion Plan may look like:

Overall Goal: To increase my energy levels for productivity in the workplace.

Long-term goal #1:   Start date: Immediately   End date: Lifelong

To build in a method to enhance and feed my spiritual self each day throughout my lifetime. To let go of any guilt I may feel about "taking time for *my* time in nature" as I need to realize this time strengthens my spirituality and gives me balance resulting in more energy, confidence and productivity.

Short-term goal #1:   Start date: Immediately   End date: Ongoing

To plan a time for my daily 30-minute walk or time in nature, ideally in the sunshine, each day. Depending on the season and my schedule, I may look forward to my walk or time in nature enjoying the beauty of the moon and the stars.

Resources required:

- Promising myself to enjoy my daily walk or time in nature without my "to do list" interfering with my promise to myself.
- Scheduling it into my daily calendar. Doing it with a positive attitude.
- All season clothing and gear: waterproof and moisture-wick clothing, comfortable runners, umbrella, mosquito repellant, sunscreen, sunglasses, hat with brim, sweaters, warm jacket, long underwear, warm socks and boots, toque, scarf and gloves.
- Portable music player, a variety of music, extra batteries, notepad and pen to record creative ideas.

Now It's Your Turn...This Is Your Life!

Begin working on your Spiritual Passion Plan by following the four-point assessment tool and creating your goals. Enjoy the process of identifying and focusing on priority action steps. You have been courageous in your personal commitment to develop your plan. Courage does not always roar; courage is often seen in simple, yet powerful actions, such as making a plan and then taking important steps to implement and evaluate how your plan has worked towards achieving your goals. When you achieve your short- and long-term goals, pat yourself on the back and be proud of yourself. When things do not work out according to plan, which is real life, do not be hard on yourself. Stay positive. Focus on your progress, not perfection. Where necessary, revise your plan and timelines and be kind to yourself.

Tips to be Spiritually Passionate in the Workplace

1. View your life with the end in mind. This will help you connect with the perspective and clarity of thought when planning your professional, volunteer and life journey. This perspective of "what really matters" will help you choose your thoughts, guide your attitudes, decisions, actions and words, and give you the gift of perspective when charting or handling change, transition and uncertainty in your life.

You deserve to live a life without regrets. Have the courage to plan your life according to what really matters in your work, life and volunteer activities. For example, choose to work and volunteer for organizations you believe in and respect. This will result in a better spiritual alignment which, in turn, will result in increased productivity and professional fulfillment.

> I hope you get a chance to live like you were dying...like tomorrow is a gift to you...got eternity to think about what you did with it...
>
> Tim McGraw, singer/songwriter

2. Let go of the joy suckers. Courageously choose and develop healthy, loving and respectful relationships. The people you work, live and volunteer with can fill your work and life with joy, positive energy and Spiritual Strength, or fill your workplace and life with unhealthy, negative energy that can break or diminish your spirit, drain you of energy, and diminish your performance, health and well-being.

You are not being selfish when you choose healthy relationships and do not settle for unhealthy, toxic relationships that erode your confidence and joy in work and life. Choose carefully and never settle for less than you deserve.

If you are a negative, toxic "joy sucking" person to work or live with, recognize this. Do not punish yourself for the past and seek ways to be positive, increase your confidence and support of others.

3. Live a balanced life to take care of your health and well-being.

> Look to your health and if you have it, praise God, and value
> it...for health is...a BLESSING that MONEY cannot BUY.
>> Izaak Walton, *The Complete Angler* (1963)

Make time for connecting with all aspects of your physical, intellectual, emotional and spiritual being on a daily basis. Include your family, work, volunteer and social life to nurture your inner self. Without balance, you internalize stress, lose perspective and feel threatened by others. Your personal and team performance may be eroded by not being as creative, innovative, productive and loyal in the workplace or in your life.

Without balance, your emotional, intellectual, physical, spiritual and relationship health in the workplace and all areas your life may be negatively affected. You cannot "snap your fingers" and instantly regain your positive attitude, balance and health. You must take a proactive approach, protecting and strengthening all aspects of your health through living a balanced life.

4. Respect yourself as well as others. Respecting yourself and others, regardless of age, gender, cultural or occupational background, title or geographic location, adds to your daily confidence and peace of mind. Respect is a core element of engaging the power of your mind, emotion, spirit and physical being to move forward with positive action in your workplace and life.

5. Work and live as a team in all areas of your life. In order to be a healthy and productive team player in the workplace and your life, you must be confident and independent. You will then be able to work with other capable, confident and independent people in companies, organizations, governments and the community.

Live the "abundance philosophy," which encourages the strengths and successes of others rather than being threatened by them. Celebrate others' strengths and successes and determine how you can work interdependently, that is, retaining your independence while working effectively together.

6. Be kind and supportive to others in the workplace. Nurture the strengths and successes of others. Recognize that we are spiritual beings living as humans who learn from every experience, giving each other "a hand up" not "a handout" in our workplaces, with our clients and all areas of our life. Being kind and supportive includes teaching, coaching and mentoring others to learn skills in the workplace that will help them immediately and throughout their careers.

7. Give voice to the importance of spirituality in the workplace and in your life. This can be a sensitive area for some people, so it is important to share your thoughts in a gentle, respectful and tactful way. As Shakespeare said, "to thine own self be true."

Do not wear a mask in the workplace or your life. Be professional, respectful and truthful about how spirituality strengthens your workplace performance. Do not be artificial; be real. If your spirituality is a source of confidence that enables you to chart the certainty of uncertainty regarding business directions, you may wish to share that insight with colleagues.

8. Do not be afraid to ask others about their spirituality. It is important to learn from the insight and wisdom of other perspectives. Even though you may know little or nothing about another culture's spiritual teachings, do not be afraid to ask questions. By asking questions, you learn and develop new insights. This understanding can help you in unexpected ways in your workplace and in your life.

I have strengthened my own understanding of my spirituality, and deeper respect and understanding for other cultures by talking with Elders from other cultures about their spiritual and community roots:

> » I will never forget the day that the late Peter Dubois, a First Nations' professional, opened the door for me to learn about First Nations' culture and tradition. While a novice in this area, I was meeting Peter to discuss career and workforce development needs for First Nations' people. I

remember saying to Peter, "It would be an honor to help with career and workforce development needs, but I have so much to learn about First Nations' culture. I have so many questions to ask. I do not want to offend you unintentionally with my basic questions."

Peter smiled broadly, his dark brown eyes sparkled as he said, "Sandra, if you ask questions because you seek to learn the truth, you will never offend me or my people. In order for us to work together and live peacefully in our communities, we need to learn and understand each other." **«**

9. Do not fear aging. As you approach your next birthday, truly celebrate the gift of another year! If your past year has been difficult and challenging, recognize that is real life. Work and life are not meant to be a smooth path. We are meant to encounter rocks in the road. These rocks may be boulders in our path.

View the rocks and boulders as learning opportunities. Ask yourself, "What lesson is being taught by this challenge? What lesson am I meant to learn?" The way in which you reframe them will turn the rocks and boulders into stepping stones, strengthening the foundation of your whole existence.

Life is too short to be taken seriously.

Einstein

I know from personal experience that life may be given to us for just a few short years. Mark Greenough, my late husband of 30 years, passed away at the tender age of 46. I remember how happy we were that Mark was able to battle his health challenge so we could be together as a family to celebrate his birthday. On Mark's birthday, January 25, 2004, I *really* understood "what really mattered."

10. Trust your intuition and wisdom. Intuition is a definite reality and there is profound wisdom in listening to it. Do not fight your intuition. Have the courage to listen to it and act accordingly. Evaluate whether your instinct was correct; you will find that it is very accurate.

11. Trust the process. Give up the need to have everything planned to the last detail. This is not a realistic approach and can set you up for significant stress in your workplace and life. Certainly, plan and identify details and expectations for your work and life's activities. However, accept and plan for the unexpected, as this is real work, real life and the real world.

Be confident in your ability to chart and manage change and transition positively. This is the key to helping you keep up your spirits, your self-esteem, productivity and healthy relationships. Challenging times, uncertainty and new developments are all part of real work and real life.

Strengthening your Spiritual Passion is a life process that will evolve and grow in its own time. Be patient and enjoy each precious moment of life and the opportunity to be engaged with meaningful work, and personal, family, volunteer and community activities.

> **Spiritual Passion is the dynamic force enabling you to live**
> **your life and soul's purpose through the connection of**
> **your intellectual, emotional, spiritual and physical being.**

May you be blessed with strength, love and joy along your work and life's path!

Sandra Greenough

Sandra Greenough's life's passion is to help others "Discover their Career Passion™ ...what they love and need to do in all areas of their life, the courage to live it & the plan to do it!" Over the past 25 years, Sandra has worked with individuals, communities, corporations, non-profit organizations, government, First Nations and Aboriginal organizations to provide leadership for career and workforce development and to help individuals of all ages to discover their life's path. She is a Certified Human Resource Professional, holds a B. Ed, Certificate of Adult Education, and is a Career & Work Force Development Specialist.

Sandra's message of vision, courage, choice and leadership reaches audiences internationally through her keynote presentations, seminars, personal coaching, articles in the press and other publications.

Her awards include being a 2005 Athena® Award recipient, 2001 YMCA Women of Distinction, (Business, Labour and Professions) Award recipient), 2001 Women Entrepreneurs of Saskatchewan Existing Member Award recipient, and 2003 and 2001 Canadian Woman Entrepreneur of the Year award nominee. Sandra is the author of the audio book, *Life Insights and the Courage to Act!* (2006).

Business Name:	Greenough & Associates Inc.
Address:	2200 Cross Place, Regina, SK S4S 4C7
Telephone:	306-789-9888
Fax:	306-761-5162
E-mail:	sandra@careerpassion.com
Web Address:	www.careerpassion.com
Professional Affiliations:	Canadian Association of Professional Speakers, Saskatchewan Association of Human Resource Professionals, Regina, Saskatoon & Saskatchewan Chambers of Commerce

Favorite Quote:
Listen to and follow the guidance given to your heart. Expect guidance to come in many forms; in prayer, in dreams, in times of quiet solitude and in the words and deeds of wise elders and friends.
—The Sacred Tree Conference, 1982

By becoming a conscious choice maker, you begin to generate actions that are evolutionary for you.

Deepak Chopra

Greg Schinkel

Unique Training & Development Inc.

Awaken the Leader Within

Y ou are a leader. Whether or not you hold an official leadership position, such as manager, supervisor or team leader, you are indeed a leader. And as a leader, you influence the behaviors of others to achieve a result. What you say to your peers influences their behavior. What you say to your children and spouse affects how they respond to you. Even as a follower, you provide leadership to your peers and your boss.

Your impact on others has a multiplier effect that expands and influences far beyond the workplace. What you say to people and how you lead by example affects people beyond their working relationship with you. When you make a positive impact on them, they will be more likely to take those positive attitudes home to their family and into the community. In turn, their positive behaviors will benefit others, and the effect will be multiplied many times over. The choices you make as a leader—and how you lead—are key.

Leaders can have a negative or positive impact; it's up to you to decide. Through words, you can reinforce unconstructive behaviors—saying negative things, gossiping and consistently complaining will bring down those you influence. Choosing inspiring words—expressing appreciation for what is going well for you and for others and refocusing them on their potential for success—can bring the opposite results. Spread good news, show appreciation for good things and watch the people around you become more positive.

Improving communication is only one aspect of a three-prong model that will help awaken the leader in you. It provides a foundation for leaders and those who choose to lead to excel. The three prongs are:

Prong #1—Pollinate: Similar to a bee pollinating flowers, spread good news and build strong connections between yourself and others. Your positive approach to life will become contagious to the people with whom you interact.

Prong #2—Communicate: Give people your full attention when you communicate. It takes significant effort to focus on people and listen with your ears and eyes. Master this and watch your influence over others increase dramatically.

Prong #3—Appreciate: Observe and acknowledge the good things happening around you. Show appreciation to people and their sense of self-worth will appreciate. Become known as a person who encourages others to reach their full potential.

Prong #1—Pollinate

Successful leaders understand that it is easier to build on positives than focus on negatives. Leaders who choose to pollinate will be able to create improvements and success for themselves and those who surround them.

Pollination is the opposite of commiseration. It is the spreading of good news instead of the sharing of misery. It seems today that we are thriving on negativity. You've experienced commiseration at work, home and school. It begins with a complaint or negative comment voiced by one person. That individual is looking for others to share in their misery. The challenge is that most of us do not feel comfortable disagreeing with the person doing the complaining. It is easier to go along. Unfortunately, the complaining snowballs and the person who started it feels that they now have a number of allies. All that attention reinforces the negativity, so they tend to spread even more of it. They begin to feel that cynicism and sarcasm are their tickets to social acceptance.

Pollination requires you to take a positive viewpoint, to look on the bright side. A person who sees life from a positive perspective is attractive to other people. Even if they outwardly make fun of it, they appreciate it deep down inside. Choose to be a person of positive influence and watch how people around you respond.

Commiseration	Pollination
Did you hear what's going on with John? Rumor is that he is having trouble at home.	We all have struggles from time to time. I'm sure John wouldn't appreciate us talking behind his back. Maybe we should be more supportive while he's going through this.
We would all get more done if Sarah didn't make as many mistakes in her work.	I wonder how we can help Sarah master her work so we all benefit?
Can you believe the e-mail that Bob sent? That's going to tick off a lot of people.	Before we jump to any conclusions, we should make sure we know what Bob was trying to communicate. You know how e-mails can be misinterpreted.
This constant overtime is stupid. The company needs to hire more people instead of heaping the work on us!	It's great that we are busy. It's better than being short of work. Our jobs are likely more secure because things are busy.
Customers are so grumpy, it's driving me crazy!	Our job is to serve the customer and do our part to making their life a little better.

Span of Influence

Your span of influence is comprised of the large group of people with whom you interact and communicate. Most people underestimate both the number of people they influence and the impact they have on others. Developing some self-awareness is the key to learning to pollinate rather than commiserate. Complete the following exercise to get a better area of how your approach impacts your span of influence. Rate yourself on a scale of 1 to 5, giving yourself a 5 if the statement describes you most of the time and a 1 if the statement describes you almost none of the time.

Span of Influence Assessment

I have a positive view of myself and the world around me.	5	4	3	2	1
I see interactions with others as an opportunity to have a positive impact on them.	5	4	3	2	1
When I speak to people, I stay positive and avoid joining in their negativity or complaining.	5	4	3	2	1
Most of the people I interact with at work would recognize me as a positive influence on others.	5	4	3	2	1
My family would describe me as having a positive outlook and influence on them.	5	4	3	2	1
Members of the community I interact with would remember me as a person who is a positive influence.	5	4	3	2	1
I know clearly what I want in my life and focus on the positive things I want, rather than dwell on the negative.	5	4	3	2	1
I understand my special gifts and talents and find ways of using them on a regular basis.	5	4	3	2	1
I have discovered a sense of purpose in my life that I feel passionate about.	5	4	3	2	1
My work does not feel like work because I love what I do and I am able to use my talents and my passions at work.	5	4	3	2	1
I take a personal interest in people I interact with.	5	4	3	2	1

If you scored 4s and 5s in most or all of the Span of Influence Assessment elements, congratulations! You are well on your way to being a positive leader to those around you. In those areas in which you scored a 3 or below, you have the opportunity to improve your leadership impact on others. Select one or two elements in which you would like to make improvements and begin consciously modifying your behavior until you achieve the results you desire. Consider returning to the assessment again in the future to evaluate your progress and highlight additional elements for future improvement.

Prong #2—Communicate

Those you lead are hungry for you to communicate at a deeper level. Shallow communication leaves people feeling just as empty after talking with you as they did before. A leader recognizes that communication is their only tool to translate the vision and desire in their mind and make it a reality through the efforts of others. Communicate well and you will enjoy greater success and achievement. Communicate poorly and watch how your stress and frustration grows, both from having to explain things repeatedly and from dealing with the disappointment of not achieving the desired results. Move from the safety of the shallow end into the deeper end of the communication pool. When you ask how someone is, be more interested in their response. The following are some powerful examples of how to lead as a communicator:

1. Take time to listen. Instead of asking, "How are you?" be more explicit: "How is life treating you these days?" Look them in the eyes and wait for a response. Leaders earn greater respect and loyalty by taking the time to communicate at a deeper level.

2. Make yourself available for others. Leaders can be distracted by e-mail, phone calls and pressing deadlines. When someone needs to speak with you, give them your full attention.

3. Listen with your eyes and your ears. Body language makes up more than half of effective communication. Leaders know that body language tends to reveal a person's true emotions and feelings.

4. Reflect and summarize to demonstrate understanding and empathy. Watch how people are drawn to you when you are able to reflect back to them what they have said. A leader who can summarize and reflect proves to the other person that they have been listened to.

5. Suspend the desire to give advice. Most people do not enjoy being told what to do. Instead of feeling as if you have to solve their problem, act as a sounding board so that they can discover their own solutions. They will be more likely to buy into decisions they make themselves.

6. Use "I" Statements. People will distance themselves from emotion by using "you" instead of "I." "You know how when someone lets you down, it frustrates you." Make it more personal by saying, "I felt frustrated because a friend let me down."

7. Share experience through stories. Because people resist being told what to do, tell more stories that get the point across. By sharing a personal experience, the other person will be more likely to accept the information and take action.

8. Avoid sarcasm. Sarcasm is when the words and the tone do not match. The brain pays more attention to *how* something is said rather than the words used, so sarcasm has a negative impact. Leaders who give people feedback in a straightforward manner will gain greater respect and warmth from others.

9. Use less e-mail, more face-to-face communication. E-mail has become a trap and an excuse for less face-to-face contact. While e-mail is effective for short, fact-based communication, leaders recognize that it is less effective in situations that require persuasion or buy-in. Face-to-face communication also gives you feedback from watching body language.

10. Tell people what you want them to do, not what you don't want. You have a greater chance at success if you focus on what you want people to do, rather than describing what you don't want.

Core Barriers That Limit Potential

Through the training and coaching we provide to managers and executives, we have discovered that there are several key barriers that can stop a leader from being fully effective as a communicator.

There are elements of your personality, thinking processes and behavior that contribute to your success and there are parts of who you are and how you think that do not support your success and happiness. Many of these strengths and weaknesses can be traced back to the impact that your parents have had on you and your experiences in life. The following are a few interesting observations that may apply to you:

Perfectionism—Leaders who have unrealistically high standards of performance have trouble enjoying what they have achieved. They cannot see excellence in others or offer praise and encouragement. Begin to recognize your own achievements, and acknowledge the improvements others make. You will then lead them to grow their performance over time and move closer to their full potential.

Comparing yourself to others—It is better to focus on achievement of your full potential than to constantly compare yourself to others. Extreme competitiveness prevents a leader from encouraging the maximum growth of the people around them. By shifting your focus, you can encourage others to achieve their full potential and be more self-satisfied.

Being argumentative and noticing flaws—Some leaders are blessed with a sharp wit and the ability to see flaws that others may not notice. While it can be handy to see opportunities for improvement, overemphasis on the negative will limit success and achievement. Begin noticing and commenting on the positive things around you. People will enjoy being in your company and you will enjoy greater leadership success.

Being soft and avoiding challenges—Leaders who avoid difficult situations and are overly concerned with what other people think about them are limiting their influence. Focus on creating dynamic interdependent relationships and stepping forward into addressing issues that demand your attention and involvement. Be confident in your ability to make a difference, and watch how people respond positively to your personal leadership style.

Your Impact in Communication

The following is an exercise that will help you rapidly improve your communication ability simply by being more aware of your actions. Under each of the following headings, list five people with whom you communicate especially in a role of leadership or authority:

- People at work;
- Family and people close to you;
- People in the community.

Positive, Neutral or Negative

Now with each person, think of a recent interaction or encounter you had with them. Rate it as positive, negative or neutral. Take a look at each one—are you satisfied with your results? How can you improve them?

Be Clear About Your Expectations

Avoid personal disappointment by clarifying and communicating your expectations of others. In our book *Employees Not Doing What You Expect*, we noted that the number one reason employees fail to meet the expectations of their manager is because they do not know what the expectations are. You may find yourself being disappointed by how others are behaving towards you at home or at work. The key question to ask yourself is, "Have I been clear in describing exactly what I want and need from this person?" A straightforward approach is better than hinting and hoping the other individual gets the point you are trying to make.

Take a moment to clarify the expectations you have of those people you deal with on a regular basis. Write the expectations down and practice saying them in a straightforward way. Then sit down face-to-face and share your expectations of others. You may be surprised to discover that you start getting more of what you want and less of what you do not want.

Prong #3—Appreciate

Your success as a leader is related to your ability to help the people around you grow or appreciate in value. In the same way that real estate appreciates in value, people you lead and influence can appreciate in value. You can train, coach and mentor people to help them gain and refine new skills that make them more valuable. You can show your appreciation by acknowledging the progress people make and the success they achieve.

Seven Tips to Inspire the Best in Yourself and Others Every Day

1. Be thankful and appreciate the gifts and blessings that surround you;
2. Say "thank you" to the people who serve you or do something for your benefit;
3. Avoid commiseration and stay positive;
4. Build others up by saying something positive about them;
5. Avoid sarcasm and replace it with positive, empowering statements;
6. Take a personal interest in others, their families, hobbies and interests;
7. Be a listening ear to the challenges that others face, and point out a positive they may not have considered.

Commit Yourself to Stronger Leadership

Awakening the leader within you requires honing your skills in the three prongs. Pollinate by focusing on the positive, connecting with people and being a catalyst for success and achievement. Communicate by articulating your messages, reinforcing the actions you desire and giving your full attention to others. Appreciate the growth and progress achieved through and by others.

As you become awake to the leadership characteristics inside you, you will begin to feel a sense of satisfaction that comes from being a positive influence on those people around you. Imagine the power of watching people achieve more than they ever thought was possible!

Make a promise to yourself now, that you will become more awake to the influence you have over others, and that you will be a leader who brings out the best in yourself and others.

Greg Schinkel

When you are passionate about what you do for a living, it no longer feels like work. **Greg Schinkel** has discovered that secret and now thrives on sharing those insights with leaders in hundreds of organizations.

Having reached more than 500,000 people through his writing, speaking, training, television and radio appearances, Greg is a recognized expert in leadership. Since graduating from the prestigious Richard Ivey School of Business, more than 10,000 people from more than 700 organizations have been positively impacted through training programs delivered by Greg's company, Unique Training & Development Inc.

Greg has served as president of the Southwestern Ontario chapter of the Canadian Association of Professional Speakers and the Canadian Association of Family Enterprise. He is the co-author of *Employees Not Doing What You Expect*.

Be sure to visit www.uniquedevelopment.com to join thousands of other sub-scribers to Greg's free bi-weekly e-newsletter and enjoy Greg's practical insights on a regular basis. Consider bringing Greg and his team into your organization or asso-ciation to strengthen your leaders and deliver transformational training and coach-ing programs to your management team and front-line staff.

Business Name:	Unique Training & Development Inc.
Address:	148 York Street, London, ON N6A 1A9
Telephone:	519-685-2116
Toll Free:	1-800-622-6437
E-mail:	gschinkel@uniquedevelopment.com
Web Addresses:	www.UniqueDevelopment.com
	www.GregSchinkel.com
	www.HowBadIsYourBoss.com
	www.BeABetterLeader.com
	www.EmployeesNotDoingWhatYouExpect.com
Professional Affiliations:	Canadian Association of Professional Speakers; International Federation of Professional Speakers; Canadian Association of Family Enterprise; Canadian Professional Sales Association

Beryl Allport

B. All Enterprise—Be All You Can Be

It's Daylight in the Swamp

Studying in the evenings during my school years just didn't work for me; however, early morning brought with it some hope of retention. My father and I were both early morning beings, and as he whistled and puttered around the kitchen starting the fire and making breakfast, to ensure that I was awake, he would tap on the stovepipe that came up through my bedroom and say, "It's daylight in the swamp."

It never occurred to me at that time what an impact this awakening could imply. You see, daylight in the swamp is about awakening all of your skills, attributes and soul at work. It is about being fully alive and awake, no matter what your work environment or role.

When you are fully "awake" at work, you experience your daily tasks, challenges and the people you meet in a new way. This translates to your entire life. Go into your vacation memory bank for a moment right now. Have you ever seen the sun rise over a volcano in Hawaii and felt the incredible energy of increasing light, a new beginning and a new day dawning? If not, you can imagine how inspiring and limitless this feels. Have you ever spent time in the wild, hiking near wetlands or living surrounded by nature? Have you ever listened to magnificent cricket and frog choruses? You can sense the harmony in the workings of nature. When you become fully awakened, you have these uplifting experiences on a daily basis, work becomes easier, and you see and connect with the best in others.

Self at Work—Awakening Passion

Awakenings can, and must, be implanted into our lives and our workplaces, increasing light and heartfelt energy for each individual and culminating into harmony for the whole.

» Benjamin Zander, the conductor of the Boston Philharmonic Orchestra, is the ultimate inspiration for encouraging and bringing out the best in others. He and the orchestra have a combined vision and each is dedicated and accountable to making it happen. In his co-authored book *The Art of Possibility*, Ben tells about his "white papers" exercise. Before each practice with the orchestra, he puts a sheet of white paper and a pencil on each music stand. The sole purpose is for the musicians to write down anything at all that would increase their ability to play at their best. If this is a suggestion for Ben himself, its value is considered and it may be implemented accordingly. It also could be as simple as changing some lighting. In the end, if each musician is playing at his or her best, the result is perfect harmony, and it is a given that the conductor will look brilliant. In this case, he truly is. «

You may be thinking, "My boss would never do this." Know that you are the leader in your life at work. Know that real leaders are not those who run the biggest corporations, make the most money or oversee the most powerful countries. Real leaders are those who live authentically—who are true to their higher purpose in even the most challenging moments. Each of us as leaders (with or without official titles), can be role models who inspire others by taking responsibility for results, keeping promises, helping others to reach their potential, and are dedicated to making the workplace and the world a better place to be.

If every person takes responsibility to live and work totally aligned with who they really are, and each plays their chosen role or instrument, the results will be enlightened organizations that are the result of the people in them.

As a personal and professional life coach, working with individuals caught up in today's corporate demands and "right sizing," experiencing depression from work-related stress, and wanting to change careers and their lives, it is clear that it is essential to stay true to who you really are and your core values. Above all, bring YOU to the workplace. Otherwise, you keep trying to fit into the mania, the materialism, the products and money-driven systems. It is necessary for individuals to search out and proactively do the interviewing of companies whose mission and values align with their own—and to not settle for less. Leaders, in whatever role they have, need to know that people are hungry for this and seeking it in the workplace.

Living in this present time and fully being aware of who you really are requires deep connection to your inner being, conscious awareness, desire, clarity, focus and a commitment to personal decisions, regardless of what is going on "out there" (externally). This will also require knowing what you really want, when you are aiming to get it, and who you want to be with. There has never been a time in history when such dedication was required for self-analysis, self-worth, self-requirements and self-commitment.

When you stay true to your inner knowing and aligned with who you really are, you become an inspiration, attracting like-minded beings. As you awaken to your own authenticity, uniqueness and greatness, you inspire with increased passion and energy. As this light glows from you, it increases, just as the daylight in the swamp awakens, and results in a shared vision of the workplace becoming harmonious. This is the ultimate intention of life on earth and must become our aim.

Knowing who you are in the midst of all of this is essential. It is easy to forget the essence of who you are in today's fast-paced world. The following are some exercises to help you rediscover your real self:

1. Your core values are unwavering, intrinsic inner characteristics that define and identify you as a person. They represent your heart and soul. It is essential that you stay true to them. In any relationship, your five top core values must be sustained. Examples could include: integrity, wholesomeness, imagination, creativity...

Write down your five non-negotiable core values.

2. Your legacy is like an obituary, something written or spoken that describes how you will be remembered when you are no longer here…and we never know when this will be. The time to "live" your legacy is when you are alive! You will be remembered for your acts of kindness rather than how much you have acquired.

Write your own legacy—one word or as much as you like.

3. Write a random profile of yourself, noting the things, activities, people and places that bring joy and passion into your life. Examples could include: continuous learning and growing, outdoor activities and healthy lifestyle, music, family life, meaningful relationships…

4. Prioritize your joys and passions by making a list of the specific things, activities, people and places that you wrote about under the previous question (#3). Put them in order of priority, with #1 being the highest priority.

Is the real you showing up about now? If so, and noting your top priorities just listed, what do you think has to change in your life (if anything), for you to support this authentic self? Note the specific life areas your priorities fall into, and then create action steps in each of these areas to ensure they happen. Be sure to give each one a specific time frame to help you to track your success. Pay particular attention to your work–life area, anything that needs attention or change. How will you take the action steps to make these changes? Also, who will be your support to ensure self-accountability and your personal awakening or success? A support network is essential as you commit to making any life change. Are there fears, doubts or total disbeliefs in your mind at this moment, saying, "How can I make such a difference?" Start living your legacy *now*, in alignment with your values, priorities and passions.

You definitely can make a difference by awakening your life and bringing light with you every day into your workplace (or wherever you are). It's contagious, and let's face it, we may not be able to change the world single-handedly, but each of us can start in our own swamp by inspiring one person at a time.

Attracting What You Need and Desire

The concept of "attracting" what you want or need may seem a little foreign to some of you, so think of your energy as being like a magnet—a force drawing like-minded people, synchronistic events, money, relationships or ideas together.

In the context of the swamp, only plants and creatures that thrive in that environment exist or are attracted to be there. Similarly, like-minded, energized people create their awakened workplace and lives.

Earlier, we identified personal heart and soul core values that are your intrinsic inner characteristics. So, too, companies have core values that define their identity, sense of character or integrity. In order to be living and working in an awakened environment, both the core values of the company and the core values of the individuals creating it must be aligned or in sync.

How to get there? Remember that like is attracted to like.

1. Identify a desire with clarity (be specific).
2. Use your five non-negotiables you wrote under question #1 of the previous exercise to see if there is a fit.
3. Stay true to you and put it out there (write it, speak it, feel it).
4. Raise the energy by staying focused on your intention and thinking of it only in a positive way.
5. Allow it to happen, trust that the perfect scenario for you is on the way (absence of doubt).

In summary, these steps to manifesting, using attraction principals, begin with you being really clear about what you want. Next, keep positive, and up the energy around your intention in any way you can. Release all doubts you may have about it becoming real. Finally, get out of the way and let it happen. You deserve it.

The speed at which the Law of Attraction manifests my desire is in direct proportion to how much I am allowing it.

Michael Lozier

Putting It All Together

The following is a personal example of how being true to my self and being open to attraction and synchronicity brought perfect alignment and success in my work life. It was an experience that felt as if it unfolded of its own volition:

» In 1996, with no thought of a vacation in mind, I received a brochure from my niece in British Columbia to attend a retreat weekend the end of September—3,000 miles away. Immediately something in me said, "I need to do this." My daughter went with me and we were introduced to a community of alternative healers and holistic practitioners, all on a "spiritual" path. I soon knew this type of work would bring all my skills, talents and goals together and that I needed to begin leading these retreats at home in the Ottawa area.

Once back home, I made the commitment. Everything unfolded quickly for this plan to work, though I knew no one doing this type of work in my area. My gut instinct told me to attend a customer appreciation event at a local restaurant where I was introduced to a woman. When I told her of my vision, she suggested I contact an acquaintance of hers who was a facilitator of retreats. This ultimately led to many synchronistic meetings, events and people.

As a result, a group evolved, supporting me on my new work path. We created a bonded team, and my vision became the vision of all involved. Then a location for our first retreat event "appeared." While driving on a country road on a sunny fall afternoon in the Ottawa Valley, I spotted a dilapidated sign that lead me to a row of cabins with a vista of almost-white sand beach for miles. Later, I met the gentleman who had recently bought this property, having lost his wife months before. His decision was to move and work here with his sons. We agreed verbally to a deal, and the retreat was in the making!

From this first retreat—with 55 participants in attendance—the numbers quickly grew, and many other successful retreats have been held. We created a team of facilitators who knew they had a role, even when that role was not initially clear. What has made it all work is being open to inspiration, possibilities and the mystery of allowing it to unfold. A combined vision, with each team member offering their own gifts and talents by choice, and coming together to create a harmonious environment has resulted in a life-changing growth process for everyone. **«**

And it all started by my own recognition of who I really am, what my life purpose is, and following the synchronicities to attract people and, ultimately, success. It is also an example of the concept of a harmonious workplace with the ultimate team effort and results. This is self contributing to the self *and* the whole.

Promoting Daylight in the Swamp

We've looked at the concept of bringing more positive energy or light into the workplace by starting with the power of you. The following are some top tips for supporting this to happen.

1. Listen actively: Everyone wants to be heard, it feels like being valued, included, recognized and supported. In active listening, you empty your own mind of agenda to completely hear what the other person is saying, feeling and meaning. If necessary, ask questions to get clarity and confirm your understanding of their needs and attention.

2. Be present: Every second of the day, we have the opportunity to be "present" or totally involved in an experience, either alone or with someone else. How often do we say such things as, "Just a minute," "I'll get to you later," "I haven't got the time right now"? There is no comparison to looking into someone's eyes, staying present, hearing and absorbing their words, and responding from the heart (whether at work with colleagues, or at home with family or friends).

3. Be in the moment: We tend to live with our energy either in the past or the future. If you want evidence of that, tune into your own thoughts. If you think about the past, the past is where your energy goes. If you worry about the future, then your energy is focused on the future and not the here and now. Practice focusing on living in the present—live and savor every moment.

4. Tune in: Poor communication creates most of the misunderstandings in all relationships. Imagine how it would feel to have constructive and sincere interaction consistently. Lack of communication also creates assumptions that are usually negative and most of the time untrue. Imagine if we took the time and made a conscious effort consistently to tune *in* instead of *out* when communicating with others. What do you think the consequences would be in your life? Try it and see how it feels. My sense is there would be major "awakenings."

5. Hear yourself: How often are you in silence or stillness and simply listening to your own inner voice, your intuition? How precious a gift this would be, to listen to and hear your authentic self! Most of the external misalignments with each other could be altered for the better if we awakened to ourselves. With practice it becomes habit.

6. Create a conscious environment: The following are some suggestions to create awakening in your swamp, using nature as a guide and creating a supportive environment that includes open space, calming colors and sounds, and simplicity. These suggestions take into consideration your three major senses—visual, auditory and kinesthetic:

- Have as much natural light as possible entering the workplace;
- Decorate with calming color tones and varied textures;
- Include things from nature—plants, artifacts, photos of natural environments;
- Clear clutter from external spaces, as this also clears the mind and emotions;
- Choose background music carefully so that it has a beneficial effect;
- Design space that is comforting and private when health or emotional needs arise;
- Choose healthy foods and pleasant eating environments;
- Fulfill your own environmental needs wherever you are. This will enhance your productivity, energy level and well-being.

An example of conscious environment was an experiment that moved executives who were rarely in their big glassed offices into a more central location while maintaining private meeting spaces, and put the employees, who sat at a desk all day, near the windows. The results apparently increased productivity, as well as morale, and decreased absenteeism, all reflecting the willingness to accept positive environmental changes and creating an awakened workplace.

7. Stay attuned to your inner self and your awakening in the workplace: If you are dealing with high levels of stress, the following are some simple suggestions to help change your energy and thinking and keep you aware of your deeper inner self:

- If driving to and from work alone, try turning off the radio and cellphone, at least for some period of time. Now you can be in a cocoon of sorts and create some valuable self-time;
- If you need energizing, visualize yourself in exact detail winning or celebrating the completion of a challenge, goal or desire;
- If you need to calm down and relax, visualize a beautiful environment you love;
- Say or sing positive affirmations that support your visualizations;
- Bookend your days: Sit in your car for five minutes before entering, or after leaving, your workplace (or any stressful swamp) just being aware of your breath and doing some deep breathing. This will give you a much increased state of calm;
- Spend time in the outdoors rather than the artificial structures we function in. Even a 15-minute walk at lunchtime shifts your energy and awakens your natural being.

One Final Note for the Swamp

Like-minded people make the business world go 'round.

Richard Zinck

For lasting workable relationships that stay secure, it is increasingly important to connect on a deeper level of core values and trust that withstands any challenges encountered—much like maintaining a marriage in this age of personal relationship instability. When you attract, or are attracted to, like-minded people with the same core beliefs, values and ethics, your team of two or many can anticipate unexpected growth opportunities. The whole is enlightened by empowering individuation. Combining individual beliefs with corporate focus involves being accountable, true to self, and at the same time committed and respectful of the whole at *all* levels.

The swamp can be anywhere; the work can be anywhere; the self is wherever you are. Your life's work is wherever you are, and whatever you are doing, at any given time. This is about bringing increased light and creative loving energy into your life, your workplace—wherever you are, and whatever you are doing.

Beryl Allport

Beryl Allport's 35-plus years of experience and cutting-edge knowledge brings unprecedented wisdom and expertise to her work as a Professional Certified Life, Business and Retirement Coach.

Beryl has served in three levels of government and has extensive experience in the specialized areas of family-run businesses, management and fundraising. In addition to business, individual, couples and group coaching, Beryl facilitates workshops, seminars and retreats. Executive Forums that focus on mastery are her passion.

Beryl has been interviewed frequently by the media and is a popular speaker. Her "out of the box" innovative and intuitive processes and topics are constantly referred to as thought provoking.

Beryl is living her passion and purpose to propel others to be all they can be.

Business Name: B. All Enterprises "Be All You Can Be"
Address: 895 County Rd. 44, RR#2, Kemptville, ON K0G 1J0
Telephone: 613-258-6893
Fax: 613-258-6894
E-mail: beallucanbe@sympatico.ca
Web Address: www.beallucanbe.com
Professional Affiliations: International Coach Federation

Believe it can be done. When you believe something can be done, really believe, your mind will find the ways to do it. Believing a solution paves the way to solution.

Dr. David Schwartz

Theresa Syer

Hospitality Solutions

It's All About Me and My Perspective

» I was at the peak of my career doing what I loved and living the life I called "La La." I had it all: husband, daughter and dream job. An admitted workaholic, I traveled the globe in what I considered a luxurious business lifestyle. Life couldn't get any better than this, or so I thought. It was 5:00 p.m. on a Friday afternoon, when a brief one-minute meeting changed my life forever. Following a company buyout, I found myself sitting in front of the new management, who nonchalantly confirmed that after 15 years of giving my heart and soul, I was out of a job. It was that simple. My perfect world was shattered. I was out of a job…I was out of my dream…I was devastated. **«**

So many of us find ourselves searching for a second chance, a new start to find that special place where we feel inspired and excited about who we are and what we do. People who feel bored and undervalued tend to hold back their energy and enthusiasm and gradually stop feeling truly alive. Well, it's time to take responsibility to live the life you desire. It is time to explore "you," to look within, think strategically and learn, "It's all about me and my perspective.   Only I am responsible for finding my passion, altering my perspective and creating my success."

If you've ever gone through a job transition or heard your internal voice whisper to you, "I'm just not satisfied with where I am!" know that you're not alone. If you're not motivated, if you're stuck in a rut, or if you don't fit in...you can do something about it. Let's stop the apathy and cynicism and take responsibility for the circumstances and our choices.

People are changing. Now more than ever, they have a desire to make a difference in both their personal and work lives. Many individuals are focused on their personal legacy. It's no longer about money and professional status; it's about creating a more fulfilling personal life while creating a more soulful workplace. It's about quality of life, opportunity, respect and gratitude.

Discovering Your Passion

Only passions, great passions, can elevate the soul to great things.

Denis Diderot

Passion is the life energy that circulates through our lives. It is finding what we love to do and allowing ourselves to express who we truly are. The more closely "who we are" is aligned with "what we do," the deeper our passion and commitment to doing it. My parents always told me, "Find what it is you love to do and then find a way to get paid for doing it; this way, you'll never have to work again."

Recognize what makes you happy and simply do more of it. This way you'll create a more fulfilling and rewarding life for yourself. Identify what stirs the creative juices within you. Persistently pursue what it is you truly love to do. When you find your passion, you'll become absorbed in the task at hand and you'll find yourself losing all track of time. You'll find yourself achieving things you never dreamed possible.

When we consider the amount of time that most people spend "at work" during their lifetime, it is no wonder that we find ourselves continually searching for a job that we're truly passionate about. The dynamics of finding ourselves is a basic motivation to living life. It offers an assurance that we are responsible for bringing personal meaning and fulfillment to our work. It also helps make a difference in the lives of the people with whom we work. We strengthen our relationships, share abundant sources of meaning, and disclose what's real and effective.

Ambition. Drive. Esteem. These words are what passion is all about. Words that describe why we bounce back from failure and have the driving force to take great risks that end in triumph.

In order to find your true passion, you have to rethink your dreams and find that special place where you feel inspired and excited about who you are and what you do. Think back about how you dreamed your life would play out. Analyze how the beliefs instilled in you over the years would impact how you defined success both for yourself and what you believed was possible in your work. Consider your beliefs and the beliefs of those who impact your life. Acknowledge how their beliefs affect your life, your economic condition and your own personal aspirations. Once you align the beliefs with the realities of the present moment, you'll be able to free yourself to explore new options.

Take responsibility to discover your passion and create the lifestyle you desire. Overcome the deterrents and broaden your scope of vision. What was once your straightforward career within one company can become a multifaceted and unlimited web of opportunities. It is time to make every day exciting and personally rewarding.

If you agree that passion is lacking in your life or in your career and you desire to bring it back, simply ask yourself, "What is my true passion? What truly motivates me? What would I do if I knew I would never fail at it?"

As you reflect on your past and anticipate the future, understand that your past was not wasted, as it was critical to get you to where you are today. Your past and future will blend together into wisdom and knowledge, and allow you to create your own unique identity.

Find a place where you can be alone and uninterrupted while you answer the following questions. Clear your mind of everything that surrounds you and focus on what you truly love to do. Listen to your own intuition. Recognize what excites and energizes you. Trust your instincts. Now sit back, get comfortable and allow yourself to do a little self-discovery:

1. What element of your job do you really love to do? Name three things you love to do at work. When you can recognize these, you'll help yourself to find your passion. Ask yourself, what's fun? What do I like to do? Don't worry about the financial rewards that go along with it. Allow yourself to dream without rules, guidelines or criticisms.

2. What are your natural gifts that benefit the team or company? List three talents that come naturally to you. If you're having difficulty identifying these, ask those closest to you—your colleagues, family and friends—those you can trust to share with you what they see as your natural talents.

3. What have been your committed interests throughout your career? Identify two areas that have been a consistent part of your life. Perhaps the industry you work in, the department you work in or the tasks you perform. There must be some significance that allowed you to pursue these interests over the years. Identify if they were built out of convenience or out of a burning desire to be a part of them.

4. What energizes you? List three areas where you get your energy. Think back to your childhood; what always excited you? Sometimes it's those same areas that energize us today. Sometimes we need to bring back that feeling of "fire in our belly" to be able to know exactly what it is that gives us our natural high.

5. Don't ask why not; tell yourself why. Convince yourself of three reasons why you should confront the challenge and take a risk. You are only trapped if you choose to be. Only you know why you should pursue your dream and live your passion. When you accept your passion, you can free yourself from restriction and enable yourself to change your life…for the better. Don't regret later what you didn't try today.

6. How can your passion help boost your career? Identify how you see your passion interacting in your career. Are you content in your workplace? Do you love it enough to still be doing it 10 years from now?

Take the time to analyze your thoughts and intuitions. Decide on the recurring themes and identify what excites you, what you're most proud doing, what's real, what's your passion. Once you acknowledge your passion, refine it. Incorporate your passion into your existence and make every day more exciting and rewarding. Do what it is you love to do. Become the person you want to be—the person you know you are capable of being. This is your opportunity to take control of your life.

The Perspective of Your Attitude

Have you ever noticed how life can be so amazing and appreciated by some, and yet so appalling and loathed by others? Why the difference? Why do some people see only the negatives?

> *The greatest discovery of my generation is that a human*
> *being can alter his life by altering his attitude.*
>
> William James

Having the right attitude is far more significant than talent when it comes to achieving personal success. Talent is important, but the right attitude allows us to conquer hardship and find the good in dire situations. We each have the opportunity to choose how we view situations. We can perceive the glass as half full or half empty. How we respond to life's ups and downs says a great deal about our attitude. We can roll with the punches, or we can punch back.

A positive attitude gives us the energy and creativity
to accept the challenges in our lives and make conscious
choices to overcome them. It allows us to view things
objectively and put them into perspective.

So what is attitude? Think of attitude as your own perception of life—the way you view your state and daily occurrences. It is the way you express yourself through your actions and behavior. Sometimes our actions speak louder than words. We say one thing but mean another. Haven't we all noticed the roll of the eyes, the pout, the smirk? Our expression and response to situations are as important as our spoken words. The way we engage others is the same manner in which they will respond to us. People can see through us quickly and know what's real and what's not.

Think of your attitude as your window to the world. Picture your view on life through your own personal window. If you maintain a clean and shiny window, you see nothing but crystal-clear possibilities. You let the sun shine in and everything is brighter and you are much more positive. If you allow your window to get dirty and remain soiled, you block your own view. Suddenly, you face a dark outlook and the negatives start to blind you. You set boundaries and limit on opportunities. Realize that you are personally responsible for your view of life and have the ability to develop and change your attitude through self-awareness.

Self-Awareness

Self-awareness is having the ability to identify our feelings, traits, behaviors and emotions. It is having the awareness to identify what triggers our negative emotions. Knowing you have the power to choose a positive attitude over a negative one is critical to your own self-confidence. What you trust and believe about yourself is essential in your outlook of life. Your attitude is the leading force within you that decides whether you succeed or fail. Are you prepared to change your attitude for the better?

Knowing yourself and understanding what steers your attitude and emotions are the keys to adjusting your attitude. You can only change your actions when you recognize inner beliefs and dialogues that must be changed. Each person is born with unique characteristics, and by early childhood you accumulate a set of beliefs about yourself, your competency and control.

With determination, you can confidently take charge of situations. Think back for a moment: Have you ever found yourself complaining about your job and voicing your opinions of everything that's wrong with it? This is a perfect opportunity to take control of your attitude. Start by first identifying what is eliciting the negative attitude. Think back to when you started. I'm sure you thought it to be the ideal position. So what changed? Was it the job or your attitude towards the job?

We can't always change jobs or the agenda associated with our existing work environment, but we can change our perception of the job and our position on certain issues. We can re-evaluate our own self-concept and take control to replace the negativity with optimism. We have the choice to respond positively or react negatively to life's circumstances. Choice is the act that puts an end to thinking about what we might do and gives us the power to achieve our objective. Every success or failure is the result of our own self-determined choices.

Awakening the Workplace

Controlling Attitude

Most feelings come and go, but every once in awhile you can be hit with an emotion at work that impairs you down to your soul. You can find yourself experiencing reactions of anger, sadness or regret. It is vital that you take charge of the negative response and turn it into a positive action. If you don't, chances are you will hurt yourself and your reputation. You will create stress, which can turn into both mental and physical agony. You *can* take charge of your attitude and change for the better.

Below are four key strategies for you to take into consideration the next time you feel negative emotions coming over you. Reflect upon the four keys prior to losing control. Let the strategies stimulate alternative actions and ideas for you as you assess the situation.

1. Talk to yourself positively. Practicing positive self-talk is very important; it assists you to achieve your goals. When you practice affirmations or use positive self-talk—including such statements as *I can, I will, I am*—you take responsibility for the direction you want to go. You effectively monitor your emotions and scrutinize their potential impact, developing a positive attitude. For example, the next time you want to pursue a promotion at work and someone tells you that you can't, talk yourself into it. If you want it badly enough, you'll find a way to get it. Don't let yourself down. It's never too late to get what you want.

2. Think three positives. Over the years as a leader, I have found this practice very effective with team members. You can channel the negative energy into a positive action. For every negative act that affects you, immediately think of three positives. It's that simple and it works. For example, I lost my job today:

- I now have sound experience from that job with which to pursue future opportunities;
- I now have the time to find my true passion and pursue my dream;
- I now have unsolicited "me" time in which I can pause and enjoy the moment.

3. Change the perspective. Make a conscious effort to change the perspective of the circumstance. Learn to reframe the situation. Replace the annoyance or resentment with gratefulness and appreciation.

>> Shortly after my company settled into its new ownership, I applied for a senior director position. I knew I had the qualifications and experience and was surprised to learn that someone from outside the company was given the job. At first it was disturbing, but I put on the professional face and turned into an ally. I gained a wealth of information and leadership skills that I could not have obtained otherwise. When I finally obtained the position a year later, I humbly knew that I had not been "turned down" for the position, but rather "coached into" the career. **<<**

4. Focus on solutions. You have the capability to live beyond any limitations. What helps get you there is focusing your mind on establishing solutions. Choose to find a solution rather than remaining a part of the problem. Focus on the possibilities within the impossible rather than trying to control the uncontrollable.

5. Prioritize the importance. Have you ever overreacted, lost your cool and blown things out of proportion? How did you feel afterwards? Embarrassed? Recognize that by prioritizing the importance of the problem and relating to it in the hierarchy of its purpose, you solve problems quickly and without much fuss. You'll discover that the situation is a minor hurdle rather than a major catastrophe when you begin to see things as much more manageable. Even "the biggies" won't seem as insurmountable as they once did.

Your attitude influences your personal and professional life. Your attitude dictates whether you are living life to the fullest or simply surviving. It determines whether you are on your way or in the way. Be strong and motivated and give yourself the confidence to move forward. Your positive attitude is the most valuable asset you can posses. You have the ability to take control of your attitude and your life, so do it!

Success

If your success is not on your own terms, if it looks good to the world but does not feel good in your heart, it is not success at all.

Anna Quindlen

Our lives each have a beginning and an ending, with much in between. How we choose to live the "in-between" is our choice. Life is filled with opportunities, hardships, possibilities and aspirations. There is no single formula that depicts personal success. We are all unique individuals with different goals and priorities. No one is born with success; it must be achieved. We must attain our own goals, build our own prosperity and earn authority.

Success means different things to different people. It is as unique and intimately personal as your own thumbprint. If you try to emulate somebody else's success, you will spend a lifetime chasing somebody else's dream. Once you can identify what will authentically make you successful by truly feeling successful, you'll be that much nearer to achieving success.

Being successful and feeling successful can be very different. You may have the fame, fortune and family, but if you aren't fulfilled walking in these shoes, then what's the point? It's important to consider what personal success looks like to you. It comes from within you, not from what your family, spouse, friends or society expect or want you to be. When you're able to identify your own personal goals and when each goal is achieved, no matter how small, then you can consider yourself successful.

Eleven Success Strategies

Success is not an event but rather an ongoing journey. Every day is a new opportunity for success. It's time to take action to progress your life to the next level of accomplishment by adhering to the following 11 success strategies:

1. Live your life with passion. With your passion in play, you break down any barriers holding you back. No matter how trapped you feel, passion can get you out. When you let passion in, you feel more motivated and empowered. You have the excitement and energy to accomplish more and the courage to doubt yourself less. You find yourself living the life you desire.

2. Have a great attitude. Life is all about choices. Your attitude is the personal choice you make about how you react and act in any given situation. Your reaction to what happens and your perception of the situation creates your attitude and how you will respond. How you live life is your choice. Choose to have a great attitude and you will choose a future that works for you.

3. Focus on what you do best. Know your on-the-job strengths and weaknesses. Focus your time on the tasks that take advantage of your strengths. Remember to focus your time on the 20 percent of the actions that produce 80 percent of the rewards, and you will naturally become more creative.

4. Take responsibility for your life. In order to direct the course of your life, you need to take control of it. Accept responsibility for where you are now and take the actions necessary to get to where you want to be. Let go of blame, hostility and pessimism, and develop positive and self-affirming self-talk to enhance your personal development and growth.

5. Establish goals and be committed. Goals and success go hand in hand. You have to set goals in order to have something to strive for. It is imperative for you to be committed to your goals by writing them down and identifying steps you will take to achieve them. Be creative; imagine there are no restrictions or obstacles in your life, you can do and be whatever you desire.

6. Be persistent in pursuing your dreams. Don't just think it, do it! Act on your convictions. Persistence is the quality of never giving up when you encounter challenges. No matter how discouraged or against the odds you feel, hold onto your dream and refuse to give up. Failure is an option, but don't be daunted. Remember to smile at the naysayers.

7. Learn from your mistakes. Understand that we can learn more from our mistakes than we can from our successes. Identifying mistakes has more impact than making them. Learning from your mistakes gives you the opportunity to grow. Aim to find out how you can try new things and determine how projects in the future can be done better.

8. Be open to change. Change is a constant in life. Challenge yourself to change, to look ahead and move on. If you are willing to alter your beliefs, habits and behaviors, you open up new possibilities for fighting your resistance to change. For change to be effective, it requires constant vigilance in order to resist slipping back into your existing routine and comfort zone.

9. Be compassionate to others. Make the effort to say and do things that take others' views into consideration. Put yourself in someone else's shoes and see things from their perspective. By doing so, you will connect with the human spirit of others and inspire compassion from them.

10. Remember to say thank you. Don't take all the credit. Remember to recognize the efforts of others and say thank you at every opportunity. This will enhance team spirit and efforts by letting colleagues know their undertakings are acknowledged and appreciated.

11. Remain humble. Do not become the victim of a self-proclaimed invulnerability. True greatness is not about titles and positions. Rather, it is about taking pride in being part of a worthy process. It is about service and humility, about being available and being accessible.

Know that success cannot be measured by material things, fortune or eminence. To me, success is a feeling of personal fulfillment, contentment and gratitude. It's about being proud of your relationships, your accomplishments and doing what you love to do. It's about going to sleep at night, knowing you did the best you could, which is something only you can determine and control. Each one of us has the power to succeed. Success is a state of mind. You must define success for yourself or it will get defined for you. The answer to finding your personal success is inside of you. Listen to your intuition. Any moment can be a victory.

Theresa Syer

Theresa Syer's impressive career spans more than two decades and includes all aspects of sales and marketing. An unapologetic optimist, she inspires and empowers audiences as one of the most knowledgeable and entertaining keynote speakers. Theresa's high-energy message tells people how to shake off mediocrity and live up to their greatness. She has an innate ability to share her contagious enthusiasm.

A successful entrepreneur, Theresa is president of Hospitality Solutions. She is a visionary who has led organizations of varied sizes in diverse industries, and offers increased sales and market penetration, and superlative customer service. Theresa is a catalyst extraordinaire. She combines her cross-functional management background with a documented record of positive change and provides leadership based on infusing organizations with revenue-centric policies and service as the top priority.

A former Director of Sales and Marketing with Sheraton Hotels, Theresa's honors include numerous Adrian Advertising Awards from HSMAI (Hospitality Sales and Marketing Association International), Sheraton Canada's Sales & Marketing Award and Sheraton Hamilton's Manager of the Year award. In addition, she was recognized with the prestigious Greater Hamilton Economic Development Lifetime Achievement Award.

Theresa's powerful message and dynamic presentation style help motivate audiences to achieve outstanding results!

Business Name:	Hospitality Solutions
Address:	1014 Riverbank Way, Oakville, ON L6H 6X1
Telephone:	905-257-2636
Fax:	905-257-3127
E-mail:	tsyer@hsolutions.ca
Web Address:	www.hsolutions.ca
Professional Affiliations:	Canadian Association of Professional Speakers; Canadian Professional Sales Association; Meeting Professionals International (Platinum Speaker)

John Eitel

Eventually Yours Corporate Consultants

Wakings! Wakings![1]

Welcome to the twenty-first century, the paradigm shift and all the vagaries of CHANGE. While the advent of the computer and Internet continue to dramatically change the world and the way we live, businesspeople know that it is having the same profound effect on how we conduct our work. Transform you must or you will be left behind! In this new environment, the office becomes "mission critical." And the difference between succeeding and being left behind is in your corporate culture.

Today's office worker will require a more intimate involvement between his own tasks and the understanding of how the business operates. This also brings the employee closer to your most prized possession...your customer or client.

Before the Internet, businesses were primarily bricks and mortar and manufacturing of some kind. Build for one dollar, sell for two and life was sweet. Management and business concerns were satisfied with large numbers of drone-like workers, in the assembly or manufacturing environment. This, ultimately, was an ineffective system, given the distance from the boardroom and the "powers that be" to where products left for shipment to the customer. Any good intent

---

[1] King Julien Lemur in the film *Madagascar*

coming from the top, was often lost in the inertia of frustration and dissatisfaction below.

The new mantra is: "For the profit of all." This is an important statement! It is the basic platform necessary in today's twenty-first century business. Because we are dealing with the human psyche, we need to take more care and have greater interest in it. This next business cycle affords us the opportunity to learn how to build new concepts about work and work relations for the outdated applications. Bottom line is that people need this shift, and it must occur in order to ensure the work gets done consistently.

For years now, there has been an unnatural buildup of anger and hostility between the employer and employee. Unnatural, because it defies human reason to want your employer to lose money or have a bad month. In countries such as Japan and Malaysia, workers understand that if the company does not make money, there is no job...at all. In those countries, government, business and workers come together on a chosen day in the year to decide on future pay and benefits. And if the employees are unhappy with the way negotiations are going, they go on "strike." But get this...it is after hours! That's right! They strike after hours to show their displeasure, but they would never do anything to disrupt the business. Because they know if they did disrupt the business day, there would be no job or they would be replaced by the new "happy" recipient standing in line waiting for their great opportunity. In these countries, to have a job and be able to, in a planned way, take care of their family with pride and dignity is not only a privilege, but an honor.

What transformed this one-time "grateful to have a job" employee into a "green-eyed monster"? You will find that the green-eyed monster felt disenfranchised. This disenfranchisement is the feeling of being outside...left out, left behind and not important enough. They feel no ownership or involvement. When people don't feel that they are part of the solution, they feel insignificant. People who feel insignificant will, possibly after a period depression or lethargy, try to be more significant. If the company does not provide opportunities for this, then people may attack something they see as significant in the organization, so they themselves can feel significant.

Disenfranchisement is energy, and like all energy, it likes to congregate. It pulls one in and becomes the channel for all things unfair in their lives. Lo and behold, the guy next to him has had unfair things happen in *his* life as well, and guess what…his lousy job stinks too! And he knows another guy who has all kinds of bad crap happening to him too, but he works in the other office. "Hey, we're meeting for a beer after work. Why don't we all get together?" And the brotherhood is formed. Stir this mixture for any period of time and you have a company that can never rise higher than the bottom half of the glass, and no one wants that.

Enabling the Environments

Employees must be made to feel that they can connect the job with their human spirit in certain safety to let it flourish. This is the critical part of the cycle. Make the office a safe place emotionally and a refuge from mediocrity. It must be a work place where "real work" can be accomplished and measured.

When people feel included, they are drawn to the job or project. It is an irresistible human requirement for people to want to belong to something. They are looking for a place to bring their passion. If the office can be that place where they can safely bring their passion to improve and succeed…you are on to something good.

> **You've heard all this before and there is good reason you keep hearing about it. It's irrevocably true. It's the universe blasting this news at you, until you get it! The question now becomes how this universal belief can be put into practice in today's office environment for the profit of all.**

Awakening the Human Spirit

Through our international work, we've learned that people are the same all over the world. The motivating and debilitating factors that drive people are the same in China as they are in Canada. They are the same with the people in Colombia, as they are in the Caribbean. Self-worth, pride, accomplishment and dignity are the necessary ingredients to bring out the best in anyone. Most people don't venture out of their comfort zone to grow, for fear of failure, shame and ridicule. These life-sucking boundaries are put in place, brick by brick, from our childhood on.

As children, our worlds are pretty small. Parents and siblings are our source of safety and wisdom. When we go to school, we soon learn that being wrong or not fully understanding something publicly can lead to laughter and the most painful of hurts: a shaming incident in your own peer group. Things don't get any easier in the messages we hear from school, TV and church. If we are constantly reinforced by the only people we know and trust that it is not safe to venture outside of what we have already learned, we won't. We can't. Unless we are willing to be wrong or corrected.

The prospect of being wrong or corrected in public sends subliminal terror messages to our core if the body and mind are not prepared for such a consideration. Enter the human spirit.

If you get this, you get it all. "Wakings! Wakings!" as exclaimed by King Julien Lemur in the film *Madagascar*. In this scene, he is telling his people to wake up to life and themselves. We are not going to belabor how wonderful the human spirit is in its greatness. (Sometimes people don't believe this statement because it sounds like the end of every movie.) So let's look at the innate human spirit—the package that we are all given at birth. We have traits and abilities that are ingrained, inherent, intuitive, typical and standard to us all.

These traits are as *intrinsic* and *unacquired* as the involuntary operation of your heart and lungs. You don't consciously tell your heart to beat or your lungs to expand and contract. They just do. So for those of you who believe you can't do anything right, you can't possibly mess this up.

The powerful will to be creative and succeed is as intrinsic as breathing…and cannot be smothered. Many have tried (perhaps parents, teachers and friends) to snuff it out, but it won't be snuffed. Want proof of that? Look to your own life experience. Do you notice how in every bad situation you always seem to make it through somehow? When we are frozen in our lives from fear of not knowing what to do next, an answer always comes up. Right? It does. Someone appears or something happens and you make some last-minute adjustment in the worst-case scenario and you survive.

So what do we know for sure? We know from our history that we are survivors.

We know that the ability to be creative and intellectually flexible is here. Unfortunately, it appears that we only use this skill under the most extreme conditions, on the precipice of life's chasms, it seems. Here is the amazing thing: Do you know how mentally agile you must be to make last-minute moves in the face of pressure and fearful outcome? It is a hundred times more difficult to ask the mind-bending questions that come with tsunami force than to thoughtfully plan your life and deal with the small changes needed.

In the great journey of life and the mastery over all that debilitates you to go forward, this is all that is needed. The sincere and accepted knowledge, that even against our conscious belief and conscious will, we are extraordinary in our unfelt, unrealized will to not only survive…but to flourish.

It's true. You don't even have to be willing to do better or to rise to your human potential. You don't have to read a book or take a course. All the answers exist in your experience, your personal history, your body and mind. Every answer that we need for the rest of our lives is on a shelf, as it were, just waiting to be taken down and considered. All you have to do is "be willing to be willing." Not even a full thought or agreement…just the acquiescence that this power is there, undeniably there, not because of anything you did. This power will take you to heights that will at some time in the very near future enable you break out into a grin that has no end and no beginning. That grin will be your soul overflowing with untapped creative awareness just hitting the mainstream to your brain for the first time without being driven by anxiety or impending doom. You will feel a small but stirring and undeniable reassurance that you have *the right stuff* and you are not in this alone.

Foundations of Success

Before we transfer this great knowledge into actual application that can be used to transform our business and our lives in the twenty-first century, we have to cover some ground rules of understanding and agree to them. In my experience, I have found that it works best to use principles of success that have stood the test of time. There is wisdom in human philosophies that endure. These are simple points that you have heard since childhood. But remember, life was designed to be simple and rewarding. These ideas have been ingrained in our belief systems and spiritual beliefs in one form or another since the beginning of time. They are faith, hope and charity.

Faith is really another word for believing. We often give lip service to the fact that we do believe; yet in those deeper darker moments when we look at ourselves under pressure, we often still don't believe…in ourselves. Ever since you could hear and feel, someone was implying that you weren't good enough, whether you spilled the milk, said something not funny (though you thought it was), got fired, on and on. And unfortunately, if they weren't reminding us, as humans we would fill these holes of doubt ourselves, which is the most destructive trait of all.

> **You are the only one who has access to your truth.**
> **You are the only one who can enter into the presence**
> **of the truth of your soul—your royal human inheritance.**

You must have faith (belief) that the force that guides your life loves you and is non-judgmental. It has taken years for me to fight through the dogma and conventional belief systems. Believe me, life is a stream with power and direction that sometimes turns into a white water ride. But as we have already agreed, somehow we always end up safe on shore. I never realized any of this until I felt how tired my arms were becoming from swimming upstream my entire life. When we learn some personal boundaries and use some natural anticipation, we find that this ride of life is indeed tailor-made for our human spirit.

Hope is the heart of the deal. People who have no hope become desperate people. Desperate people do desperate things. Hopelessness is the ultimate reason people give up on themselves. Hope is borne out of belief (faith), encouragement and truth. Hopes turn into dreams, and the mind is designed to transform those dreams into a plan.

Charity is all about gratitude, intention and expectations. You have heard it all your life in some form from Sunday school to the wisdom of a grandparent. Why?

Awakening the Workplace

Because it is the truth. Undeniable and irrefutable truth! Charity is all about karma: You reap what you sow. You get what you give.

Encouragement and empathy are human experiences we can share. When you intend in your soul to do well and make a contribution, people feel it coming from inside and will respond in a surprisingly warm, open manner. This is about sharing something very valuable with another human being that costs you nothing. Because your heart is pure in intention, because you are sharing the human experience with someone, even on the phone, you can *expect* respect and care from those around you. It will happen. What goes around comes around, no more so than with intent. Intention is energy; and energy is power…real power! Liken it to dynamite. If it is used properly, mountains will move; if used selfishly, you risk blowing yourself up. There may be moments of uncertainty. Here is where your faith comes in. Be patient and listen for the lesson and the answer.

What's in It for Me?

Back to business. How do we make the application of all of this to the workplace known as the office? Well again, because we are dealing with human beings in a business environment, we have to answer the question, "What's in it for me?"

This may seem like a selfish question, but it is not. Everyone from the lost boy to the President has to ask this question. People only become involved in or passionate about something when they get something back. So asking the question "What's in it for me?" only ensures that you have identified something worthwhile for your effort over and above the money received. There will be an abundant opportunity to make more money in the future, but the experience that will get you there is here now.

From a management standpoint, answering these hard questions keeps the company honest. Committed and focused employees always looking to reach their personal gains in the job can do nothing but benefit their employer and shareholders at large.

The Employee

The employee is by far the big winner here! Just by listening and soaking up all the information possible and making it their knowledge and experience, the office can be our place of refuge from all the vagaries of our lives. This is a place where we can start registering small victories that will multiply and create the foundation for our future success. The following are a few guidelines for employees:

- Never take on more that you can do or understand. Don't set yourself up for failure. You must remove the attitude that you are working for "the man" or the establishment.
- Learn everything you can about the job and about your company. This is an opportunity for you to go and get paid to learn. It is your mission to absorb every bit of information you can out of the intelligencia of your company and make it yours.
- Be good at your job...a good reputation as a diligent employee can get you more money and many more opportunities.
- When you know "why" something is done, you know everything. Knowledge and experience are the natural benefits of life and asking the question...why? This is very important to remember.

Look at it as having to master tasks before you will be given other, more lucrative and challenging tasks. Put all that energy into something you know you will be successful doing if you just learn when it is offered. Done properly, you will learn not only the vast capacity of your capabilities, you will also learn how to handle people (co-workers and supervisors). Your new attitude will not only be noticed, it will be felt.

That is all business is in the end: communicating experience and vision through a relationship of truth and trust.

If you are in an environment that does not allow this kind of openness and future...make plans. Know what you are seeking clearly in your mind and go and find it. When you move forward with intent, you put the request out there to the universe. Be prepared, and watch what you pray for: Success has a way of coming in waves.

The Manager

The keeper of the corporate culture is the manager. It is here that the delicate balances are weighed. It is here that the web of confidence, wonder, hope and respect is woven for the employee to flourish and the company to prosper. The manager ends up being the most important factor in a company beyond the product or service it provides. The manager's job is to make sure the president's message gets to the market through the employees, and to instill in their staff a will and drive to see "how good can we make it," not just a job done.

The office has to be a *safe* place for employees to come. A place for them to be creative and know that "nothing ventured, nothing gained" is acceptable. They must feel safe to bring their experiences from other jobs and life to the business. They must feel that they are recognized for their effort. Overtime is more money...recognition is priceless.

The idea here is to intrigue employees with "hope." Hope that they will be wiser and more capable after listening to your instructions. Hope that there is a reason to learn because there is something in it for them. Prove that their life experience is valuable and see that they have something to contribute because we are all in this together. The following are some ideas to energize you, as a manager:

- Offer acting supervisory positions to up-and-comers. Begin to show interest in people who are putting in an extra effort. Let them know they are an important cog in your business wheel, and that if their tasks are handled with an honorable effort, there will be more opportunity for them.

- Share with employees the reasons why they are performing a task, no matter how menial it may seem. Employees who know why they are doing something, feel included enough to think outside of the box. It takes both comfort and courage to think outside of the safety of rules and regulations. When you share an office dilemma and real concern for something systemic at a daily meeting with your staff, they will surprise you with the solutions they come up with; but they must feel part of the solution.

- People need to feel good about themselves and included. Reward does not always have to come in the form of money. A kind word of recognition for an effort put forth can go very far, especially for young people with ambition and tempered direction. Employees have to own the experience of working for you. They must admire your fairness and openness, while respecting your boundaries of proper office deportment. Overwhelming them with instruction and your brilliance will make them doubt themselves, which causes disenfranchisement…and we go backwards. Developing employees is a gift. It's not always easy, but that is why you get the big bucks (smile).

Properly forged, the office environment is an easier place to manage. The staff, with you, set a higher bar for excellence. They then virtually manage themselves, and once the template is set, anyone who does not fit in will pop up. If they are a drag on the office and you see them being reprimanded by their peers…you are there! In Japan, they call it "the nail that sticks up." Hammer it back into place or remove it. It will be clear when it should happen. It is good to be a little generous with time to allow the employee to fit in, but if the time comes when it is clear that he or she doesn't…make the change.

The President

Presidents and CEOs of twenty-first century companies and organizations have to work smarter rather than harder. Choose managers to carry your message from you to fully engaged employees, all working for the same thing: success.

Division or a confused message from here to the vice-president or management level will crescendo down into ultimate chaos. Trying to unwind that mess will make you old and grey by the time it is determined who really said what. Be sure that your VP and manager can carry your message clearly.

Today's president must surround themselves with intelligent and loyal specialists who understand human dynamics. Today's president must acknowledge that they are caught up in a business transformation and become a student again. Intelligent leaders would be foolish to let the grandiosity of past victories lead them into the global market thinking that nothing is new. Everything is changing from the source of supply (global) to the demands of the new consumer (post-boomer). Never before has it been so lucrative and easy to identify ripe target markets. This is the time for experienced open-minded venture capital to clean up.

The Office

In its most clinical sense, the office becomes a laboratory, offering a pristine environment for the implementation of the business plan, and providing the conduit for the message or product to come from the boardroom to the street. In its most romantic sense, the office becomes an ethereal environment of truly mystical human potential and self-awareness, working one success at a time. The office must be a safe, secure environment—a sanctuary and intellectual refuge. You will be amazed how the right people will gravitate to your business when they can test, try, fail and succeed with their bold creativity. At the same time, it can't be a country club for the "great thinkers" where ideas never land.

Companies are valued on market access, profits and the ability to grow to the next level. A properly run company with everyone pulling in one direction costs less in real dollars to operate because everyone knows it is essential to be accountable. Companies that run smoothly grow more quickly and are noticed by possible "takeover" interests. Even smaller companies with powerful infrastructure and a "going forward" attitude are being acquired at very impressive multiples, improving purchase prices by the millions.

In my mind's eye, I can see Frank Stronach, chairman of the board of Magna International, Inc., speaking 25 years ago on Bay Street (the financial Mecca of Toronto) and the "bank boyz" laughing up their sleeves and into their coffee cups as he explained that he had created a generous ownership plan for his employees. The management and employees believe they are in it together at Magna Corp. What was laughable to some 25 years ago is the status quo today. Welcome to the twenty-first century. In this century, the ground is moving, sometimes a little and sometimes a lot. What was once standard no longer exists, and what we once feared the most now seems to work the best. This new enterprise requires your valuable experience, your good intentions and a sense of adventure.

Remember, if nothing changes…nothing changes!

John Eitel

John Eitel is a popular writer and speaker on both the domestic and international corporate scene. Together with Partner/Global Marketing Director, Yazmina Rawji, John explains "what drives the market" in human terms. His strategies help direct the consumer, corporation and advisor on global transitioning matters. John believes that human communications are the hallmark of success in the future. Sales are simply the application of the message and answering a need. Even in the world of global high-tech, the relationship is king.

John is co-founder and president of CallthePlanet, a Voice over Internet Protocol (VoIP) company. From idea to start-up, CTP is established and successfully operating in over 70 countries with 11 employees worldwide.

John's 30 years of business experience include global marketing, telecommunications, international corporate planning, venture capital, and business turnaround. John's anecdotal comparisons make him a dynamic speaker and writer with a quick and easy wit. The message is: *If nothing changes…nothing changes!*

Business Name:	Eventually Yours Corporate Consultants
Address:	912 Solem Street, Azusa, CA USA 91702
Telephone:	626-327-8365
Fax:	626-334-0103
E-mail:	info@johneitel.com
Web Address:	www.johneitel.com
Professional Affiliations:	Member of the National Speakers Association (USA); Canadian Association of Professional Speakers.

Joanne McLean, CPCC

Soulzatwork™ a division of tsc inc.

An Invitation to Lead With Grace and Dignity

Leadership is a sacred calling and a great responsibility. The current world is challenging each of us to lead with greater consciousness for our fellow employees and for society at large. You don't have to be a leadership guru to figure this out. Simply look at the state of a number of larger public and private corporations. There is a desperateness for inspiration and for the creation of a culture that truly honors difference. There is the need for a place that promotes connection and calls for courageous leaders to challenge complacency and to act with integrity.

Embrace the potential to realize a new kind of power in your leadership by leading with grace and dignity...always. In this chapter, we'll look at four key elements to assist you in doing this:

1. Becoming more self-aware, including emotional awareness;
2. Creating inspiring relationships that are honoring;
3. Staying real during the tough times—with grace;
4. Being truly courageous while creating your leadership legacy.

In this chapter, you will have the opportunity to look at your current state of being, and then embark on shifting from your status quo. You will take away a renewed appreciation that within you is the capacity to lead even more powerfully than you do already. We are going to look at "getting real": getting real with yourself, getting more connected to your emotions, noticing your impact on others (and checking to see if it matches your intent) and consciously choosing to lead authentically from who you really are…no matter what.

A Better Way

There *is* a better way. And guess what? It starts with you. There will always be great challenges, and you always have choices about how you will lead. As a leader, you hold it all: the formation of organizational culture, the inspiration of people, the outcomes of business, and finally, the commitments to multiple stakeholders—a tall order for leadership, and definitely not one for the faint of heart. You've risen to your position as a leader because you have achieved results and are considered a bright and intelligent person, right?

Organizations put people in leadership positions because these people have made a valued contribution and the organization wants to leverage that. Many who are made leaders, though, are so focused on achieving specific goals, they lose sight of the impact they are having on people, despite the fact that clearly the only way these goals are going to be met is through the collective efforts of those being led. In order to achieve real success and generate the greatest return, you must capture the imaginations, the hearts and the minds of the people you lead. In short, you better get what it means to really harness all of the human energy and resources available to you, if you want to lead your organization to achieving optimal success.

So what do grace and dignity have to do with a better way of leading? Let's look for moment at the meanings of these two words:

Grace is the quality or state of *being* considerate or thoughtful. In a spiritual context, it also has a connection with a higher power providing divine assistance.

Dignity is the quality or state of *being* worthy, honored or esteemed.

Both of these words are situated in the context of "being" as opposed to "doing." Take a moment to reflect on how you rose to your current position of leadership. It likely has had more to do with doing (i.e., achieving results) than being. Yet, now that you are here, your greatest ally for powerful leadership is how you "be."

You have the biggest opportunity of all with the people you lead. You can compel them, repel them or hold them neutral. So you have a choice: Do you want to inspire them to do their best work, stall them by being indifferent, or encourage mediocrity through negative interactions? I would assume you want to create the best possible outcomes for your organization. Yet, without consistently reflecting on what your intentions are as a leader, "stuff" simply happens. You hold the potential for your workplace, its people and its results to be extraordinary. Simply permit yourself to consciously engage aspects of leadership that might otherwise remain dormant within you.

To begin with, take a moment and ask yourself these questions:

- What if I consciously chose to lead with grace and dignity *always*?
- What would be possible for me, the people I lead, and the organization I serve?
- What would it cost me?
- What would be different in my way of leading, if I chose grace and dignity?
- What would be hard for me about leading this way?

Note your responses, as they will provide wisdom as you continue to explore new possibilities for your leadership. And know this:

Wisdom is intuitive knowledge of the truth.

Element #1—It's All About You: The Self-Aware Leader

You know it is a funny thing, this focus on self. Many of us are taught from an early age to focus on others, and we don't want to talk about or think about our own needs, desires or even our behaviors sometimes. Yet, as a leader, until you are clear about who you are, what you value, what you want to affect, how you impact others, and whether you lead from a place of fear or inspiration, you are not at the top of your game. My experience suggests that until we get it right within ourselves, we cannot possibly create the best in our relationships with others or in the culture of our organizations.

So, how do we achieve this state of self-awareness? One might argue that with more than 60,000 books on leadership and management, providing tips and techniques about how you can be more effective, get better results and be more inspiring, that we simply need to visit a library or bookstore. Is that all there is to it? I say no. We tend to rely too much on what others say about how we should lead and not enough on our own inner wisdom. This inner wisdom holds amazing gifts for each of us, if we take time to do the work on ourselves first. And it does take time, it requires reflection, and we must give ourselves permission to be vulnerable.

The most powerful ally a leader has, is not found in a book, but within oneself. The invitation is to access your inner wisdom and natural strengths, reclaim them and fully express them in work and life.

It can be unnerving to allow yourself to be exposed as you begin to unfold your truths, and discover the places where you are not acting in alignment with your values and strengths. Having witnessed people struggle with this leadership challenge over the past 20 years, it is clear to me that leaders can be assisted in their development of self-awareness, by helping them to understand their authentic selves and align their business practices with their values. This inner journey of leadership addresses clarifying values, accessing their natural strengths, passions and purpose (each of which may have become estranged from them during the climb up the corporate ladder), and then learning how to leverage all of these elements in service of the organizations they lead and of themselves. With this inner learning and wisdom, leaders "show up" from their real place of power. Working from their leadership soul, they are best able to inspire and create a culture of trust, commitment and clarity of purpose for all.

In the spirit of believing that you have tremendous leadership wisdom within yourself, let's begin from where you are now. Reflect for a moment on how you currently operate as a leader and ask yourself these questions:

- Despite my knowledge of what it means to be a powerful leader, what behaviors do I manifest that have the potential to net my organization less than optimal results? How is this making me feel?
- What are my top 10 personal values? Write them down. How do I honor them today? Are my behaviors in alignment with my values? Where are the gaps?
- What are my top three strengths? How do I use these strengths daily? Where

am I not using them to their fullest? What gets in my way? How important is it to be fully playing to my strengths? What are the costs to *me* when I do not play to my strengths?

Make a note of your thoughts related to these questions. This is the first step in creating more awareness of your current state. These are only a few questions of many that you could explore to become more self-aware. A crucial first step in shifting any behavior is simply noticing what is presently occurring and what it is creating for you and others.

Integrating Your Insights

An interesting observation about people: they don't always act on what they know. So knowledge, and making personal changes as a result of that knowledge, are two very different things. You have lots of information at your disposal. You may even have some new knowledge from your personal reflections right in this moment, and still not incorporate it into how you choose to behave.

Leaders are often well-read and knowledgeable about what to do, in terms of leading, and yet they get in their own way. You may get in your own way because you have "blind spots" that preclude you from shifting the status quo. The good news is these blind spots can be turned into "sweet spots" when you remember that this work of leadership begins with your own self-awareness! Once you are more consistently self-aware, you can fully focus on your unique strengths. We must invest time to understand our strengths, hone them and use them, and not default to emulating someone else or unconsciously slip into exhibiting behaviors that are not in alignment with who we are.

This journey of leadership is definitely an inside job! To do this inner work, you need to treat yourself with compassion (always remember, grace and dignity for yourself first). This kind of self-development can make you feel vulnerable at times. And paradoxically, when you stay in the discomfort of the vulnerability and are truthful with yourself and others (even in the face of opposing views), you create and display a new kind of power. A power that is rooted in humility. Vulnerability, power and humility provide a wonderful triad for great leadership.

Those leaders with whom I have worked, who have committed to really looking at their own barriers, doing the work of clarifying their values and strengths, and holding themselves accountable to continually practicing and observing their evolved way of being, are experiencing extraordinary results. And what they notice is that when they slip back into an old way of behaving out of fear, or feeling a loss of control, they find they get more stressed and do not get the best results with their people or the organizations they serve. They also have noticed that they are far more engaging when they are behaving from who they really are, for example:

- a leader who despite being in a culture that values charismatic, extroverted energy, is now very effective and confident with a quiet, more reserved style of leadership; or
- a senior executive accountable for a major re-engineering process who now always takes time to talk with team leaders one-on-one to help them transition to a new business focus, even in a fast-paced culture that is hard-focused on bottom-line results.

These leaders are renewed in themselves, they are more confident and they are achieving better organizational results, with ease. And their people love them! When you are willing to learn more about yourself, discover your blind spots, and reorient yourself to behave in ways that are more in alignment with who you really are, you are awakening the real leader in you.

Your vision will become clear when you can look into your heart.
Who looks outside, dreams; who looks inside, awakens.

Carl Jung

Emotional Awakening

In order to grow as an awakened leader, you are called to become more emotionally aware. As you are more emotionally aware, you also become more skilled at recognizing, acknowledging and supporting the needs of others, and creating more connected relationships. This opens up huge potential for designing more productive work relationships that are empowered and rooted in real shared accountability for the outcome, whether that is a challenging conversation or a project deliverable. As your awareness grows and you hold yourself more accountable for your own behaviors, you naturally hold others accountable for their behaviors in a new light. More than ever, in today's business world, extraordinary results are achieved through strong relationships. And this can only happen fully when you are first in an emotionally aware relationship with yourself!

There are a number of well-known experts in this area of study, including Daniel Goleman and Reuven Bar On. Bar On describes emotional intelligence as a set of non-analytical skills and competencies that influence one's ability to succeed in coping with life's demands and pressures. These competencies include such attributes as inter- and intra-personal behaviors, the ability to manage stress, adaptability, sense of control, outlook and initiative. The inner work of the awakened leader includes being emotionally aware. Emotional awareness is typically not the type of learning and training you get as you progress into more senior roles in organizations. And yet, in order to be effective in creating a positive culture, inspire others to deliver their best, and embrace and leverage differences to attain better results, you need to both respect others and be tuned into your own and other's emotional barometers. Take a moment to reflect on the following questions:

- What is your ability to read your own emotions in any situation? How aware are you at any given time about what you are feeling?
- What is your ability to think and act independently in challenging situations? How would you describe yourself under pressure?
- How do you manage stress? When is it most difficult for you?
- What are your strategies to find new ways of handling challenges and problems? Where do you get stuck?
- What are your beliefs about control—of situations, of people?
- How would your people say you are at empathizing with them and their situations? What is your belief about empathy in the workplace? About showing emotion in the workplace? About dealing with someone who is eliciting an emotional response to something in the workplace?
- How would you rate your sense of optimism? And what about your ability to take initiative, even in the face of ambiguity?

These questions are not intended in any way to take the place of an in-depth assessment of emotional intelligence; rather, they are intended to have you pondering your own emotional barometer.

Element #2—It's All in the Dance: Creating Inspiring Relationships

Leadership that is built on the foundation of grace and dignity requires you to acknowledge that you are not alone, but rather, are in a dance—the relationship dance. The sooner you begin your own dance, where you'll move with your own vulnerabilities, fears and strengths, the better equipped you'll be to enter into the dance with those you lead. If you are going to lead fully, you gotta know the dance!

As you know, dancing is more pleasant when you feel graceful and dignified. All dances can be wonderful expressions of energy, some of them may be wild and some may be peaceful. And if you want to be accomplished at the dance, you should know the steps and then be committed to put them into practice. So let's get started. Think about this:

- What are you trying to create with your team?
- What do they need to know about you and what you want from them?
- When was the last time you had this kind of conversation with your team?
- What do you need to know about what they want from you?
- How do you know that you are in a productive relationship with your people—in service of the organizational goals? What is your check-in process with them?
- How do you handle your people, when you don't know the next steps?
- What is the biggest dream for your team? What is the worst disappointment you could imagine?

As you continue to create an emotionally aware relationship with your team, you will experience an enhanced ability to effectively manage with consistency, even in the challenging times. There are a number of principles that I have found particularly helpful with my clients as they learn to more successfully navigate the relationships in the workplace, and elsewhere too. In order to be in a productive and energizing relationship, there are a number of behaviors you need to exhibit as the leader, and also be willing to call forth in your people:

Maintain mutual respect—even in the face of differing opinions or perspectives. Honor each other for what you bring to the relationship, even in the face of challenge.

Hold the bigger picture—the work relationship is about creating something bigger than any one of you. As the leader, you hold up the mirror of possibilities for the team. You carry the vision and the dream, always.

Withhold judgement—in the service of allowing all aspects and expressions of difference to be heard, and keeping communication open. This requires a lot of self-management on your part. At some point, decisions need to be made, and it is critical to the health of the relationship that everyone feels their voice is considered. You do need to make independent decisions sometimes.

Put the team first—since you are not in this relationship alone and you are responsible for inspiring the team to work to the good of the whole organization. You are accountable for everyone understanding that the team comes first.

Demonstrate heart—if you demonstrate heart and lead with compassion, grace and dignity, this invites others to do the same. When people know you care, they care. Ensure that your heart-filled intention always lines up with your behavior. When this happens, people trust you. When trust is present, magic happens. In the relationship, all parties will feel free to take risks, in service of new solutions. When heart is present, the relationship dance will be more fun, more committed and more abundant.

Think about these questions:
- What would be different if you led with your heart?
- What scares you about that?
- What is exhilarating about leading with heart?

In a final reflection about the dance of the relationship and its connection to your leadership, contemplate the following:
- What are three things your employees would say about your relationship with them today?
- And about the dream… How is your team engaged in the dream? Where is

their opportunity to be more directly involved? What are the risks in giving them more ownership? What are the potential wins?

- What is your strategy to build and nurture the relationship with the team? With each member of the team?
- How do you feel about more inclusion of your people? Pay attention to the places where you feel uncomfortable. What is this about?

Your role is to make things happen through people, in order to best serve the organization as a whole. In this segment on the leadership dance, we have touched on the potential for delivering better results through a dance with your people that is engaging, inspiring, fun and sometimes vulnerable. Success is dependent on you getting work done through your people. They rely on you to know the steps and take the lead, even when the going gets tough.

Element #3—Grace Under Fire

Courage is an act of leading through the unknown.

Having great relationships with people at work is easier when things are on an even keel. It's when the going gets tough that really defines the type of leader you are. When it comes to extraordinary leadership, I say that when the going gets tough, the tough get grace. Obviously, you need to be tough-minded, and you need to lead with heart and compassion as well. Intellectually, you know that when the heat gets turned up, you need to stay calm and unwavering. When faced with such uncertainty, however, what one knows is the right thing to do isn't always sufficient. You need to summon the deepest part of yourself (accessing your values, natural strengths, your emotionally aware self) to show up with courage and commitment to lead fully through the situation.

These are the times when people are watching most intently, needing encouragement, and believing that you can manage what needs to happen in a way that demonstrates personal honesty and preserves organizational integrity. This will be your finest hour of demonstrating grace and dignity. There is no higher contribution you can make as a leader. So when you are faced with great challenge, and perhaps the unknown, how will you be? Think of times of great challenge in your life and reflect on how you handled yourself and those around you and the decisions you made. Review and answer the following questions:

- Think of a difficult situation you faced as a leader. How was your behavior different or the same, compared to how you were in your normal state of day-to-day actions? What was most striking about how you were in the crisis situation?
- How could this way of operating help you in your day-to-day way of leading? What might the lessons be for you—from your handling of a crisis?
- Where was your focus in the crisis? Where is your focus typically on any given day? Any differences, similarities?

What I have experienced with a number of my clients who have faced challenging leadership moments, is that when a crisis hit they either:

- moved into a mode where they were clear, focused and operating for the greater good of the situation, resulting in actions grounded in their values and natural strengths. And at the same time they were able to pay attention to and learn from the external environment and be open to new creative possibilities. That is, they were open-minded; or
- they became focused on what was happening to them, and they led from a place of protecting their own interests. They acted often in isolation of others' input, and after the fact, they realized they were not playing from their strengths but from a place of trying to control the outcome at all costs.

There are lessons in all situations, if you are prepared to learn from them without judgement. On reflection, you can leverage what worked, learn more about yourself, and contemplate how you would choose to react in a similar situation the next time.

Element #4—Creating Legacy by Leading With Courage

In each moment of leadership, you are creating your legacy. Legacy is not something to put off until you are old and retired (or simply tired). Rather it is about consciously creating it each day as you lead with courage through uncertainty, new challenges, change and wonderful possibilities.

- What is the legacy you are creating today?
- What would your people say about your legacy?
- What is your impact right now?

Legacy is an enduring gift of the soul.

You always choose how you will lead—every day, and in every situation and every conversation. Carry this mantra with you and it will help you when facing unknowns, new challenges and even some of the simple day-to-day situations that may unnerve you. Tell yourself, "Walk through this with grace and dignity." This mantra is calming and helps in focusing. Believe that you can demonstrate those attributes at your most difficult times, and serve as a model for how you want others to act.

So, I ask you now, what mantra will you use when facing your biggest challenges? You have an amazing opportunity to design greatness that will result in extraordinary results for you and those you lead. Simply surrender to the voice of your inner wisdom that calls you to lead courageously with grace and dignity, paying attention to what you know about yourself, and the mark you want to leave every day.

You have all you need. You can choose to be the leader that our world needs today, one who is self-aware and inspires people. One who develops relationships that foster good work and delivers excellence. And finally, one who leads courageously and creates legacy daily, in service of the whole organization. Just begin.

Joanne McLean

Joanne McLean is a certified executive leadership coach who helps leaders "get real." Her mission is being a catalyst for leaders in accessing their authentic leadership power and leveraging their strengths. Joanne motivates and teaches leaders to captain their lives and businesses in ways that produces fulfilling, sustainable results, while doing it on their own terms. She believes that leadership is a sacred calling and has great respect for those who choose to lead.

Prior to launching Soulzatwork™, Joanne's 20-year career journey took her into senior roles in global corporations (high-tech and pharmaceutical sectors) in employee health management, business development, marketing communications and strategic human resources, including leadership development, succession planning and executive coaching. This diverse business experience has allowed her to work strategically with senior executives and also with senior management at the operational level. As an entrepreneur, Joanne has owned and operated her own fitness and wellness consulting business and worked as an external business and health consultant for numerous organizations.

Joanne understands that leaders must act fast, work with integrity and get results. She works with leaders and their teams to create a better way to work, resulting in enhanced business outcomes and amazing work relationships.

Business Name: Soulzatwork™ (tsc inc.)
Address: 2546 Burnford Trail, Mississauga, ON L5M 5E3
Telephone: 905-567-5009
Fax: 905-567-5305
E-mail: joanne@soulzatwork.com
Web Address: www.soulzatwork.com
Professional Affiliations: The Coaches Training Institute (global community leader),
                          Canadian Management Centre (faculty member)

It is your attitude, not your aptitude, that determines your altitude.

Zig Ziglar

Terri Knox

Speaker/Life Coach/Author

The Power of Service...Inside Out!

"**A**re you always this friendly?" This question was asked of me on a daily basis while working within the airline industry for well over 20 years. As a flight attendant and then a customer service agent, I felt that every shift I worked was one of the best times in my life. One day while sitting with a dear friend and lifelong mentor, Louise, I mentioned that I could not imagine another job that I'd love as much. Then I noticed her smiling... "What's so funny?" I asked. She replied, "You have said that about every job you've ever had."

Having a roadmap to follow your dreams and attain goals is essential in today's busy world. By applying the user-friendly tools in this chapter, positive results will ensue. You will recognize how these many proven tools, tips and strategies are designed to turn on every individual's internal "success magnet." The information in this chapter is designed to fit with the reality of our day-to-day challenges in any industry and in our personal lives.

Working on these suggestions is not just an option for those who wish to enjoy the journey called life. We can't afford to miss the information train, which passes our doorstep every waking hour. To accelerate both success and the achievement of personal goals, we must connect to our limitless potential from the inside out.

As a novice speaker many years ago, I began by believing that I was going to deliver speaking engagements on customer service. It took me approximately three sessions to recognize that service or teamwork is not a teachable thing. It comes from within. It's like trying to start a car without a key. Yes, we can hot-wire it, but it takes a lot more work and at times can be dangerous! I am aware of how hard it is to change ourselves, but it is impossible to change someone else. Rats, you may say, but the reality is, we must change by choice and not force.

Go…With Attitude!

> *The greatest discovery of my generation is that a human being can alter his life by altering his attitude.*
>
> William James

William James wrote these words 100 years ago and they are just as meaningful today. One of the most overused words in today's society is "attitude." Yet, it remains the most critical element in superior service, teamwork, success, financial outcomes and personal relationships. I always get a kick out of people who think that if they don't open their mouth, no one will know what their attitude is. Wrong! Any one of us can walk into a bank or an airport and know 50 feet away who we *don't* want to serve us. I tend to automatically propel myself to the individual who looks like they enjoy being there and want to help me.

Researchers have found that employees who like what they do are much more efficient doing their job. Call it amazing or even impossible, but when you have a good attitude about yourself, you tend to age more slowly and certainly more gracefully. Think of walking around with a scowl all day (even if it's internal). There would be permanent creases etched on your face. This is not about walking around with your teeth dry from smiling. Know that your eyes dance with energy when you celebrate who you are. One of the biggest freedoms allowed us by God is our ability to choose how we move forward in the world.

You have heard from many that attitude is the foundation of our lives. When you have to work with colleagues you would never choose as friends, have an aggressive boss, or grouchy customers, you should recognize that this is not your choice. Your choice lies in how to respond to them. You can choose to work for someone else, and let the possibility of a new boss be worse. You can also choose to develop coping skills. Use your encounters with difficult people and situations as learning experiences that allow you to acquire coping skills and life strategies.

The same can be said about customers. When nasty customers happen, recognize that they have been placed in your life to teach you something. Don't waste those lessons. Many of my shifts in the airline industry were in the lost-baggage department. I loved it! I was given many opportunities to change a situation where a passenger was upset with our organization, and by responding to their needs, I ended up having him or her walk away with a renewed sense of service from our airline…sometimes even without his or her bag! Was it always easy? No, as a matter of fact there were times when it was virtually impossible for the customer to have a positive outcome. You can still give service while not being able to fulfill someone's requirements. The following is an example from personal experience:

» One day, I found myself totally lost en route to a speaking engagement. I was trying not to panic as I was searching for the location. I like to get to any function early so that I can ground myself and be totally prepared. What I was not prepared for was to get lost; so when I saw the RCMP officer stop me and approach my car, I was elated and told him so. I actually thought he knew that I was lost. He was surprised that I had not realized that he had pulled me over because I was speeding.

I now went into recovery mode, explaining to him that I was running late and on my way to speak to a group of city employees, including some RCMP officers. He asked me where I was headed, and upon telling him the location, he indicated that I was totally off-track with my directions. He offered to lead the way so I would get there in time. I was ever so grateful!

At the parking lot, he helped me unload my manuals and briefcase. As I was about to depart into the building, I stopped to thank him for his help and gracious spirit, and he asked me to hang on while he wrote me my ticket. I was in total shock, assuming that I beat the ticket while having him direct me to my location. He indicated that if I was in a hurry he could deliver the ticket to me while I was doing my session. I opted to wait and he handed me a $125.00 speeding ticket. My point here is that while I was not intending to receive a ticket, this officer still did his job while providing me with exceptional service! «

Most angry or upset customers, or even fellow colleagues, are looking for you to enter the ring with them during difficult situations. Making the choice to mentally cross the line and join their team, whether you would personally pick them as team-mates or not, is important. A key thought to remember is that we are ambassadors of the organization that pays our wages, and only we can have the ability to ensure that customers come back by demonstrating our passion for service and empathy.

Your attitude can make or break a toxic environment within the workplace. If you are feeling overwhelmed and helpless, it is more difficult to remember your choices. When we let our emotions rule us, we tend to choose desperate and negative responses to situations. When you believe that you are not in control of your destiny and are feeling stressed and overwhelmed, a vicious circle of toxicity can be created.

We own our attitude and it's up to us to take responsibility for that! We can and most certainly will have bad days, yet our attitude will determine how long we stay there and how many people we hurt along the way.

Research indicates that there are two basic reasons why people work: money and motivation. If you work only for money, you probably don't like your job. Even though working for money alone is not constructive, working for only motivational reasons is also not suggested. If you only work for motivational reasons, you are probably not doing a good job. One good example is the airline industry. If you work for an airline solely because of the benefits, such as travel privileges, it is unlikely that you will be fully committed to your job and customer. The true key is finding balance. Ah, there's that word everyone seems to be spouting these days…"balance."

How do you obtain balance? It is not accidentally found, but created. You must clear the path so there is room to discover and develop skills, which will ensure the balance you are looking for. Dr. Phil has said, "You will never change what you have, if you don't change what got you there." If you are in a job where all you find is fault in others—most individuals can't even imagine that they may have anything to do with it themselves—then you will be stuck in your own negativity. Balance will never occur.

If we were to do the math, we would recognize that we spend many of our waking hours as an adult at our place of work. Can you imagine that so much time can be misused when we are not utilizing our full capabilities, by staying in a job/career that we loathe? Here is a great example of someone making the most of a job that we tend to undervalue:

>> This is about a man who works as a taxi driver. This man wears a suit every day to work. He personally takes pride in what he does. When someone gets into his cab, it's clean. He offers a variety of hot and cold beverages in thermoses. The newspaper of the day and magazines are at hand, and he asks what type of music a customer would like to hear. Can you image the pride this taxi driver experiences every day while on the job? There are business people who book him throughout the year, and many times he has to disappoint them, as he is already booked! The result is that he ends up making much more money, including larger tips, while creating a way to love his job. <<

Rejuvenate in the Workplace

Our attitude and thinking create the life we live and the job we do. There are powerful—yet simple—ways to realign, readjust and open ourselves to a new attitude in the workplace. The following are some of the most effective ones that you can begin to incorporate today:

Own and be in charge of your emotions. Have you ever considered how we are not always in control of our feelings? Yes, many times we may not like where we are or what is happening at work or even in our homes. The greatest thing we can recognize is that we are always in control of our response to any situation. This is where real professionalism and growth comes into effect.

In the workplace, there are many who suffer from bitterness syndrome. Unfortunately many do not celebrate another's success or ability to provide great teamwork or service to others. I believe this is mostly due to the fact that they themselves feel intimated by those who are positive and looking for ways to make things work rather than focusing on negativity.

A negative attitude can be toxic, and if we allow ourselves to get caught up in this atmosphere it becomes problematic for all, including the customer. Stopping the emotional treadmill long enough to get off and re-evaluate can be a great start. Instead of putting so much energy into trying to keep an unhappy experience alive, you can certainly turn it around as a learning experience. Start by recognizing your self-worth.

The greatest gift anyone has ever received is his or her life. How we live our life is also the greatest gift we can give back. When we compare ourselves to someone else, it makes us either better or worse. This is not positive reinforcement. I know that there are some people who have amazing jobs, jet-setting all over the world while making huge amounts of money. Not for even a moment would I suggest that I would not hesitate to have that sort of job and or career. The reality, however, is that I do not have that sort of life or job. The most important thing that we can do is recognize what we have. Once we realize where we are, we then can make a conscious decision to ensure that we commit to making it the very best, both personally and professionally.

Be aware of your values. Too often individuals do not take the time to reflect on their personal values. Have you ever wondered what your values are? Take a moment to write down some of your core values that are important to you, including ones that are significant in your particular industry or workplace. These may include honesty, commitment, integrity or being of service to others. Writing them down, allows you to visualize them and become more committed to your values in your life. Also, take a look at your behaviors and see if they match what you have written. For example, if you value being a team player, how do you do or not do this? If you have a sense of guilt or shame as you reflect on how you express your values, it can be an indication of the distance between how you perceive yourself and what you are actually doing.

Commit to your customers. I once had a colleague who had a hard time with my commitment to friendly service to customers. Internally, he thought that I was "kissing up" to management. This was far from the truth, as my rewards were greater than what I ever would have received from management. One day as we were walking along a corridor, he told me that within three months I would have the same negative attitude he did. He indicated that, by then, I would be jaded by passengers and the public. He continued to say that this service and energy that I believed in and delivered would eventually run out. He never understood that my service to others fueled me and also enabled me to continue filling my service tank. The more I gave to customers in service, the more I received in return.

Believe that most people are inherently good. If I were to give an estimate, I'd say that 97 percent of all people are good people—or they have the ability to be. Three percent are chronically miserable! Who are they? They are the ones who do not have a good thing to say about anyone, anywhere, any time. Sometimes they are even ourselves!

Here is a strategy for removing yourself from the influence of the negative 3 percent. When we encounter a nasty individual, they are usually looking for a response. If we react and give them what they are looking for, it reinforces them and encourages their poor behavior. Not reacting and killing them with kindness is the key. Avoid syrupy or even sarcastic responses to them.

Don't give your power away. Bad things can and do happen...just don't give the power of your behavior away. Your attitude will always be up to you. You wear it every minute of every day. Your attitude about whatever happens to you is always up to you!

My sense of delivering amazing service to any industry or job in which I have been employed is somewhat selfish. You see, I love giving knock-your-socks-off service and also making that happen internally with colleagues, as it has always been a self-motivator for me. I love the quote from Erma Bombeck: "When I stand before God at the end of my life, I would hope that I would not have a single bit of talent left, and could say, 'I used everything you gave me.'" I believe that talent happens within you. Let's not waste our talent; instead, let's begin to use it all up. It's like renting a car with the gas plan included. We try so hard to use up all the gas, driving as much as possible, because we have already paid the price. Let's not pay a higher price by not using the amazing talents that we all possess.

Developing an in-service attitude. If that means being the best that we can be, while enriching the environment within the workplace, why not indulge? Now this can also create problems within the workplace environment, as there are many who do not like watching a fellow colleague enjoy themselves, especially if they themselves are unhappy. I have encountered many a colleague who has given me a very difficult time within the workplace. There were times that I was moved to tears, but I never gave them the power to take my personal passion from me. The most important thing to remember is that no one can take away from who you are, and the only thing that you are in control of is your response to him or her.

There is no more noble occupation in the world than to assist another human being and help one succeed.

Allen Loy McGinnis

Take personal accountability. Most workplaces tend to have internal staff issues. This is common and does not have to be thought of in a negative manner. The causes can be many, including jealousy, differing personalities or other internal problems. When this sort of atmosphere exists, it is imperative that each employee takes personal accountability to ensure the customer is not affected. An important message to all managers is that the employee is the biggest commodity of any organization. Treating staff in a manner that reflects how employees should treat customers is critical. Can you imagine what would happen if you kicked a dog in the backside and then tried to pet it? There is a high probability that it would bite you. It always amazes me when companies expect employees to perform at their best, when in fact the employees themselves have not received excellent service from management. This is another reason to reawaken the workplace from within. Looking for ways to enable people to work together, especially during trying times, will create healthier internal relationships. With this sort of healthy attitude, difficult situations have a better chance to work out, instead of being fueled by negativity.

Professionalism…always. I have numerous customer service stories, which I share in my delivery as a speaker. If I have a bad story, and unfortunately, there are too many of them, I never give the name of the organization—even if after the session someone privately asks me. There are two reasons for this: 1) they are not there to defend themselves, and 2) it is very unprofessional! I also think that we, as consumers, ought to carry more responsibility than most of us do. When there is as complaint, I believe that it's our responsibility to let that particular organization know. Call it laziness or just plain not interested, but the truth is that we have no right to be telling others about a negative experience when, in fact, we have not let the organization know first. Once we have shared our experience with a company, then telling others would be more acceptable. The very least we can do is give an organization a chance to respond first. In doing this, you might have a different story to tell.

If this sounds like a healthy idea to you, can you imagine if we were to incorporate that sort of behavior with fellow colleagues when things go awry? Far too often

Awakening the Workplace

we go directly to others when a problem occurs between two or more staff members. More often than not, most of the staff hears of an incident before the individuals who were part of the given scenario. If we can remember to focus on our job rather than reacting to stories and gossip, the synergy could be amazing in most workplaces.

People often need to be reminded more than taught. Of all the inventions occurring every day, I personally believe that I need to be reminded more than I require teaching. This does not mean that I do not celebrate growth through learning, but often we must go back to the basics before we can move forward with the new.

In conclusion, the following are some proven methods and tips that can be posted in any lunchroom or on a family fridge, enabling us to be reminded at all times.

Ten Tips to Rejuvenate the Workplace

1. Invest in yourself. We need to believe in ourselves or we cannot deliver service to others.
2. Identify your personal and professional goals. If we fail to plan, we plan to fail.
3. Professionalism…always! No matter what your job function is, you are a professional.
4. Attitude is the main ingredient to being a professional. The greatest freedom we will ever have is the ability to choose our own attitude.
5. Being a team player enables us to understand that every employee is each other's customer. Without internal customer service, there can be no external customer service.
6. Job satisfaction is crucial to self-motivation. Learning to motivate ourselves is the key to continuous improvement.
7. Stress is necessary and common in everyday life and in the workplace. How we handle change will determine how much stress we will have.
8. Communication skills are essential to customer service. Being an effective listener is the most crucial of these skills.

9. Complaints are necessary to improve customer service. Complaints allow our organization to become stronger and better.

10. Believe in you. You are the most valuable commodity you will ever own. Your success, both personally and professionally, starts with and ends with you!

A strong positive mental attitude will create more miracles than any wonder drug.

Patricia Neal

Terri Knox

Terri Knox is an insightful, innovative and high-energy speaker, author, trainer and life coach. Using introspection and humor, Terri assists her audience members to live each day with passion and purpose and to maximize their unique God-given potential on both a personal and professional level. Her main areas of expertise include personal development, self-image, teamwork and customer relations.

Nominated Female Entrepreneur of the Year, Terri, through her successful company, has been bringing inspirational keynotes and seminars to a wide variety of clients in every sector across North America. She accumulated a wealth of experience while dealing with the public in her 22 years in the airline industry, and as coordinator of education and training for the tourism industry.

Terri believes that in today's competitive economy, the key to increasing your bottom line will be super exceeding customer service expectations. She also believes strongly that positive reinforcement enhances skills. Recognize your power within!

Terri has released two CDs: "Tools for Success" and "More Tools For Success" and is co-author of *You're the Boss...of You!* and a contributor to *Expert Women Who Speak... Speak Out,* Vol 2.

Business Name:	Service Enhanced Training
Address:	#30 3512 Ridge Blvd., West Bank, BC V4T 2X5
Telephone:	250-768-1140
Toll Free:	1-877 488-1171
Fax:	250-768-8897
E-mail:	terri@terriknox.com
Web Address:	www.terriknox.com
Professional Affiliations:	Canadian Association of Professional Speakers

It is better to believe than to disbelieve; in so doing you bring everything to the realm of possibility.

Albert Einstein

M. Beth Page

Dream Catcher Consulting

Connecting Heart and Mind: The Secret to Being Awake and Fully Alive at Work

Has the "real you" become buried by the tyranny of the "should haves," "could haves," and "what ifs" of your work environment? Are you dissatisfied with your current work experience? Do you see your work as joyless, stress-filled and burdensome? Is this the way you want your work to be defined?

At a recent conference, organization development practitioner and leader in the field Tony Petrella invited all of the participants to view their work as "sacred." Imagine what life would be like if you believed with all your heart and mind that the work you were doing was deemed invaluable…indeed, priceless. Imagine how you would feel if your work was treated with the utmost respect. In other words, that your work was viewed as sacred. This chapter will offer you six top secrets that will give you the power to make *your* work sacred and to help you become fully alive at work.

Secret #1—Clear Your Path

My heart is afraid that it will have to suffer," the boy told the alchemist one night as they looked up at the moonless sky.

"Tell your heart that the fear of suffering is worse than the suffering

itself. And that no heart has ever suffered when it goes in search of its
dreams."

Paul Coelho, *The Alchemist*

The path taken to being fully alive and awake at work is a lifelong journey. Like any journey, there will be days when things run smoothly and everything seems to click, and then there are those days when nothing goes right and you are faced with seemingly unimaginable roadblocks.

All of us have experienced the highs and lows within the workplace. Whether it be a conflict with a colleague at work, a job change, an angry supervisor, an overall change in a company's business success or its merger with another company, each of these situations impacts us greatly. The excitement we had for going to work each morning may no longer exist. The confidence and job satisfaction we once enjoyed no longer holds true. The discovery that a work situation we once had a great deal of passion for is now unbearable can shake us to the very core of our being. What do we do?

We have several choices available to us. We can "put in time" and wait unhappily for retirement. We can seek out the pessimists, the doom-and-gloom co-workers, and complain that things aren't like they used to be. We can suffer in silence, or we can clear the path of this "mindset" and take the next step in this lifelong journey. We can try to rediscover the passion, the self-understanding and the creativity within us, because all of us deserve nothing less than a sacred work experience.

This requires work, and the challenge may seem insurmountable at times. This is the journey; this is the fork in the road; this is the path less traveled. This is a journey of discovery to the very core of you. Maintaining the momentum for this journey involves periodic check-ins to ensure that the path ahead is being cleared.

Yes, there will be challenges to face as you seek to be fully awake and alive at work. There will be times where all the circumstances seem to be in your favor, everything seems to be "just right," yet you still can't seem to move forward. Why?

One of the reasons for this inability to move forward could be competing commitments. In their *Harvard Business Review* article "The Real Reason People Won't Change," Robert Kegan and Lisa Laskow Lahey identify competing commitments as, "a subconscious hidden goal that conflicts with their stated commitments." For example, if an employee expresses a commitment to getting ahead in a particular career, yet they have not applied for or completed a certification required for career advancement, there may be a competing commitment that is operating along with the stated commitment. Perhaps the employee believes that the new position will require longer working hours and will take away from precious family time. A variety of competing commitments can operate when an individual's stated commitment appears to be at a standstill.

Simply put, ask yourself this question: Have you ever prepared yourself for a change and yet, "for the life of you," taking the first step seemed impossible? What was holding you back? Fear; a lack of self confidence; or was there some hidden belief within you that was competing with this commitment? In clearing the path so you can be fully awake and alive at work, you must find the answer to this question. *You* are your greatest resource for your personal success.

Sometimes we use self-protection strategies to protect ourselves from personal risk. Try to uncover the strategies you use, knowing that this is a lifelong process. Be compassionate with yourself as you begin to clear the path.

Exercise

- Describe the strategies you use to protect yourself from risk.
- Who can help and support you to uncover alternative strategies?
- What is the one thing that is preventing you from moving forward to being fully alive and awake at work?

View your responses to this exercise as positive considerations, rather than as obstacles to your goal. You can now decide how much power these considerations have in determining your outcome. As you move forward in this self-discovery, you'll become more and more aware of the choices you are making.

Secret #2—Make Intentional Choices

Each day we make choices. Each day the series of choices we make informs the world around us about what is important to us. Too often our day is spent "putting out fires," and reacting to situations. How many individuals say their day, "just happened" to them? An element of today's workplace is about being able to adapt to the change that takes place, and it is also about making deliberate, intentional choices. Intention is a powerful tool for bringing meaning to your day.

Intentional choices clearly state what is meaningful and important to you. Being purposeful with your intentions offers the benefits of bringing increased energy, focus and power to your life. Stating your intention for your day creates increased personal energy. Your personal focus is clear to you. You claim your personal power as you make intentional choices.

Take a few moments before the workday begins to decide what intentional choice you will make from your heart that will give your day more meaning. Making this statement of personal intention serves as a guidepost for the rest of the day. For example, your intentional choice for a particular day may be to express your appreciation to your colleagues, co-workers and service providers or any others you encounter along the way. It is far more energizing and rewarding to begin each day consciously aware that you are expressing appreciation and acknowledging the positives, rather than beginning each day ignoring your co-workers, complaining about your supervisor or focusing on the negatives. As you bring your intentions to life at work each day, you will feel more alive at work.

Take a few moments and complete the following exercise each day for the next several days to increase the intention you bring to your work.

Exercise

- Create a meaningful personal statement that will guide you through your day.
- Check in periodically throughout the day to see if you are living this intention.

Living life with intention is not counter to getting the job done. It becomes a way of life. It creates space for work to get accomplished and for doing it in a way that aligns with your heart. Living life with intention is one way of claiming power. The power comes in "how" the work gets accomplished. The "how" can be unintentional or intentional. How do you choose to work today?

Secret #3—Own Your Personal Power

The third step to creating a fully alive work experience is to reclaim your power. True choices are made from a place of personal power. Operating from this level has very little connection to traditional trappings of power, such as title, financial status, elected status or leadership. Power is discovering *your voice* and using it to express the wisdom of your heart.

Reflect on the times in your life when you have diminished yourself and your personal power. Were you silent; protecting yourself; playing it safe? Remaining silent or playing it safe are choices that may render you powerless. If you don't actively participate in the conversation, how can you ever hope to get your needs met, much less claim your power? Do not give your power away through your silence. The choice to claim your own power at work, in life and in relationships with others may be as simple as expressing yourself openly rather than remaining silent.

The essence of power is something we experience at the heart level. Your wise heart recognizes the authenticity of someone who is operating from their core. What we admire in the other's heart is also in our own or we would not be able to recognize this quality. Consider the messages you offer and receive through your interactions with your family, friends, colleagues and community. Authentic power is available for you to claim. The choice is yours.

Exercise

- Reflect on someone in your life who has been a significant positive influence.
- What are the qualities of the individual that are memorable for you?
- Did you experience the person as powerful?

The choices we make each day tell others and ourselves what our priorities are. If you care enough to get angry about an issue, protest a wrongdoing, grieve a loss or celebrate an accomplishment, you are telling others that these situations matter to you.

Often, the difficult relationships we experience in our lives are linked in some way to a past experience that has a strong emotional connection for us. In choosing to be fully awake and alive at work, one of our tasks is to ensure that we understand fully what triggers this negative reaction. Often our choices in our difficult relationships are being driven by old historical relationships. Perhaps the awareness of the links will help us make choices today that are based on current data rather than old history. We can choose to make a fresh start.

By owning your personal power you can speak up and use your voice to take ownership for getting your needs met; you can represent yourself fully by being open with others; you can take a stance to assert your opinions with a colleague; and you can participate more actively in the decisions being made in your work environment. As you claim your personal power, you will experience your work as more dynamic, fulfilling and rewarding because you will be more involved and invested in it.

Secret #4—Identify Your Essence

There is a vitality, a life force, an energy, a quickening, that is translated through you into action, and because there is only one of you in all time, this expression is unique.

Martha Graham

The fourth step to creating an awake and fully alive work experience is to identify your personal essence. Essence is the special mix of values, beliefs, past experiences and motivations that are your unique blend. Your essence is the very core of your being. Your only responsibility to yourself is to nurture the essence of who you are so the real you will thrive in your life and your work.

According to John Monbourquette in his book *How to Discover Your Personal Mission*, "the principal factor in discovering our mission is self-knowledge. Whatever form our mission takes is rooted in each individual's identity." Creating quiet time to get in touch with your essence, to grow in self-knowledge and to nurture the voice inside of you that yearns for a more meaningful and sacred work experience becomes a key secret for bringing the essence of you to your whole life.

The following breathing and visualization technique will help you as you identify your unique essence. Begin by placing your feet flat on the floor and letting your hands rest comfortably in your lap. Close your eyes and take three deep, cleansing breaths. Begin to visualize yourself in a sanctuary of your own creation. Take a look around, where are you? What is around you? Is this place familiar to you? Note the details of your sanctuary. There are no editors or inner critics present in this sanctuary. This is a safe place. You are here with the inner voice of your wise self. You can return to this sanctuary anytime you wish. When you are ready, open your eyes and complete the following exercise.

Exercise

- Describe a time that you were excited about going to work. Describe the work experience and what you loved about it.
- How did you feel at the beginning and end of each day?
- Describe an achievement or accomplishment that you are particularly proud of from this work experience.
- When you reflect on the essence of being fully alive at work, what feelings and values come to mind for you?

Identifying your essence is a lifelong journey of discovery. The demands, responsibilities and commitments of the external world may silence the voice of the inner core of your being. The benefits of focusing on this journey to your inner core will be an increase of abundance, vitality and energy; and the work experience will become richer as you align your choices in your work with your unique essence.

Keep this list of feelings and values nearby as you continue through the rest of this chapter. It offers you some guideposts to the qualities that need to be present to nurture your essence in your work. You may wish to add other qualities, values and feelings to this list as you continue to read. This list may also open the window to the many paths available to you for being fully awake and alive in all aspects of your life.

Secret #5—Develop and Acknowledge Your Cheering Section

We all have angels guiding us...they look after us. What will bring their help?... Asking. Giving Thanks.

Sophy Burnham

We go through our lives with cheerleaders who support us on our journey. Perhaps a teacher, a friend, a work colleague, a life partner, a child, a mentor, a career coach, a boss or a neighbor has taken an interest in our lives and has propped us up when we've experienced tough times. The people who support us play a crucial role in our journey to be fully awake and alive at work. Whenever an individual changes, adjustments are made to accommodate the change by friends, family members and colleagues. Expressing our appreciation to these important people in our lives helps them to know that their presence and support is an important part of our journey.

If you are seeking to have a larger cheerleading team, begin to take ownership for letting people in your life know how they can support and help you with your efforts. This secret is crucial for sustaining momentum for your journey. Cheerleaders can play a variety of roles: supporting you by being there to celebrate your accomplishments; providing a listening ear when you encounter obstacles; reminding you of how your history has prepared you for this current journey; loving you through the times of uncertainty; offering you the benefit of expertise that you are lacking; putting you in touch with different resources to help you succeed; or being present for you when you need to be distracted. Every member of your cheering section will play one or more of these roles. You can have as many members in your cheering section as you wish.

Surrounding yourself with a cheering section will provide you with support and help you to sustain the momentum for your journey. As you work, you will have reminders all around you of your intentions and your commitments to yourself as your cheerleaders offer you encouragement.

Exercise

- Identify the people in your life who support you.
- Who is on your list that you need to acknowledge personally?
- Are there other people you would like to invite to be part of your cheerleading team?

You help your cheering section participate and support you as you become more of you. There is another unintended benefit that your cheering section experiences when you are fully awake and alive. It's not something you set out to do, and yet it happens anyway. What happens is that you become a role model for people in your life. In choosing to be awake and fully alive at work, people in your life observe you behaving in a way that honors you and the people around you. You become an inspiration to others.

Secret #6—Make Your Commitments

The moment one commits oneself, then providence moves too. All sorts of things occur to help one that would never have otherwise occurred. A whole stream of events, all manner of unforeseen incidents, chance meetings and material assistance come forth which no one could have dreamt would appear. I have learned a deep respect for one of Goethe's couplets: "Whatever you can do or dream, you can begin it.
Boldness has genius and power and magic in it."

W. H. Murray

This is a call to action to you the reader. It's an invitation to live life from the inside out. In choosing to live life from your internal core, you become the most powerful person you can be. You become the essence of you. There is only one you in the universe and you are being invited to be nothing less and nothing more than who you are.

Your commitment is to you. It is a sacred pact that you make with yourself. No one but you will know if you are living your life from the inside out. You matter.

Your life matters. How you choose to bring yourself more fully into the workplace is up to you. It may be through intentional statements, through openly expressing yourself, or through a change of workplace. You determine what conditions are necessary to be fully awake and alive at work and determine how to bring these conditions to life. This is the time to listen to the wise voice of your heart. You have all the tools you need. All that is missing is action to support your desire. The power, the choice, the actions all rest with you. Choose to have your actions represent the essence of you.

For too long the message has been to park our emotions at the door before entering the workplace. When that message is conveyed, the outcome is that people do not bring their hearts to work. In last season's final episode of "The Apprentice," Donald Trump expressed concern to one of the female apprentices who showed heightened emotion in the boardroom. He stated how much he disliked any signs or expression of emotions. Her quick reply was that she had seen many football players express emotions when they had won the Super Bowl and she felt that if the players could express powerful emotions, so could she. At the end of the show, she was selected as the successful apprentice for the coming year. Heart and emotion are the core of passion, creativity and innovation. Who wouldn't want these qualities influencing the success in any workplace, in the boardroom and in global organizations?

Bringing all of ourselves to work is possible. The choice is ours to make. In the next exercise, make your commitments in writing.

Exercise

- What three changes will create space in your life for being fully alive at work?
- How committed are you on a scale of 1 to 10 to each of these changes, with 10 being 100 percent committed to the change?
- What is holding you back from initiating the changes?
- Who do you need to help you move forward with the changes?

Congratulations! It's on paper. You've written it down. Already the work is in progress. If you want to anchor it further, read your three changes out loud. You are the witness to your creation. The amazing thing is that by writing your three changes down, you have created space for forward momentum. There is a significant change going on right now. You have made your intentions clear. The final step is to take actions that support your intention. You have embarked on a journey of self-discovery that will continue to offer you the opportunity to make intentional choices, claim your power and identify your essence.

You are the author of your life. You are invited and encouraged to write a great story. Open yourself up to the adventure that is waiting for you as you embrace being fully alive and awake at work. Your adventure is sacred, unique and precious.

There is a traditional African-American spiritual song that captures the essence of the message of this chapter. Perhaps you are familiar with the tune. If so, feel free to hum a few bars as you look over your responses to the various exercises in this chapter. Better yet, sing it out loud. It goes something like this:

> *This little light of mine, I'm going to let it shine.*
> *This little light of mine, I'm going to let it shine.*
> *This little light of mine, I'm going to let it shine,*
> *let it shine, let it shine, let it shine.*

As you move forward to the next steps on your journey to being awake and fully alive at work, let *your* light shine.

M. Beth Page

M. Beth Page is a writer, speaker, coach and consultant dedicated to reintroducing people to their greatness. Through her work, she is an advocate, leading the revolution of "alive" people who are connected to their essential self.

Beth is the author of *Done Deal: Your Guide to Merger and Acquisition Integration* (ISBN 0-9739130-1-0), and is co-author of *Working With Heart: Your Guide to the Power of Choices in Work and Life* (ISBN 0-9739130-0-2), which will be published in 2006. Visit www.authenticitypress.com for more information.

Beth has a Master of Science in Organization Development from Pepperdine University, a Master of Science in College Student Personnel from Western Illinois University, and an undergraduate degree in Psychology from Carleton University, Ottawa.

Business Name: Dream Catcher Consulting

Address: Suite 554, 185-911 Yates Street, Victoria, BC V8V 4Y9

Telephone: 250-483-6729

E-mail: beth@dreamcatcher-consulting.com

Web Address: www.dreamcatcher-consulting.com

Professional Affiliations: Canadian Association of Professional Speakers, Vancouver (Chapter board member for 2006), British Columbia Human Resources Management Association.

Favorite Quote:
If you have it in you to Dream, you have it in you to Succeed.

—Alwyn Morris

Audrey Ciccone

Human Perspective Consulting Ltd.

Creating an Authentic Workplace

Another Monday morning. You pull yourself out of bed, get ready for the day and make the long commute to work. You grab a coffee, plunk yourself down at your desk and start checking e-mail. Feeling engaged in the workplace? Perhaps not.

If this is the vibe you feel in your workplace, chances are a number of your colleagues are feeling the same way and some are already looking for new jobs. Employees today are much more likely to leave a company than wait for management to address workplace morale and corporate culture. They don't have the time and patience for unaddressed issues, corporate politics, shifting priorities and poor leadership.

Companies have the best intentions of providing a stimulating workplace. To the executive team, the company's vision, mission and priorities are evident. The difficulty comes in effectively communicating this vision to the rest of the company and developing the business systems and practices to embed it into the corporate culture.

Nothing irritates an employee more than hearing about their company's vision and values at meetings or in corporate literature, and then not seeing it applied consistently in the workplace. Instead of the vision and values being inspirational, they are ignored, and serve, in turn, to demotivate employees. Companies neglect a significant opportunity to increase employee performance and, ultimately, the company's profitability, which comes from engaging their employees' commitment to a shared vision. Vision and values can't be just words on a page; they need to be evident in every aspect of the business. Authentic workplaces use a company's vision to ignite the passion and motivation of their workforce.

The Authentic Workplace

Every company has a rhythm—the pace by which business happens. The rhythm is made up of multiple simultaneous events which occur hourly, daily or weekly in various parts of the organization. Sales people interact with clients, orders are submitted to suppliers, managers monitor results, decisions are made, databases are updated, money comes in and money is drawn out. While the rhythm is affected by external forces that can speed up or slow down the pace, the tempo is set by the company's management style and business practices.

There is authenticity in your workplace when the means and methods you use to conduct your business are congruent with the corporate vision and values. Authentic workplaces build their business around a core vision. This vision forms the foundation for how the company functions: its people, organizational structures, business systems, ethics, leadership style, management practices, customer service and external relationships. When the leadership abilities and business systems are in sync with the corporate vision, you have the beginnings of an authentic workplace…everyone working in rhythm toward a shared vision of success, with leaders setting the tempo through their style and practices.

There are two foundation elements that build an authentic workplace: 1) organizational structure, and 2) people.

1. Organizational Structure

There is no secret formula for creating a great workplace or a one-size-fits-all approach to developing an engaging corporate culture. Every company has a different passion, a different purpose and unique values. Articulating this vision and using it as the touchstone for your corporate strategy, your decisions and your expectations is the key to building authenticity in your workplace.

Creating an authentic workplace is important regardless of the size of your business. Small and medium-sized companies can have the advantage over larger ones because the executive members and leaders generally have a more hands-on connection with their employees. These businesses also have fewer politics and can react more responsively to change. As with larger organizations, though, creating a visionary and values-based organization must start in the CEO's office. Only a visionary leader can ensure that company-wide practices support the company's vision over the long term.

Too many companies continually get caught up in the stresses they have built into their culture through policies, rules, micromanaging and legacy practices. They lose sight of what makes them successful: a clear vision and the passion for meeting the needs of the customer. Building an authentic workplace involves cutting through the noise to uncover the heart of the business and reigniting the passion that drives the organization's success. Getting back to basics is not a new management practice, but it can be challenging, and it will take time, patience and perseverance to strip away the old systems, expectations and other barriers to become authentic. It has to be what you know in your heart is the right thing to do, and you have to be committed to it, or it will not be sustainable. There are four key themes that need to be woven into the way business is conducted to ensure you have a solid and consistent foundation upon which to build an authentic company: a visionary focus, values, communication and trust.

Visionary Focus

Imagine piloting a boat without a clear destination in mind. The journey may be interesting and relaxing or fraught with peril. One thing is certain, though: the journey will take you a lot longer than if you had planned your course ahead of time. Companies without a vision can also be fun and adventurous places to work, but they will fail to attract financing, investors, dedicated employees and leaders with the drive to make things happen over the long term. If you don't know where you are going, how can others help you get there? Few people are willing to invest their careers or job security in a rudderless ship.

A company's vision is the reason the business exists irrespective of profit. It is a broadly stated, forward-looking looking goal of what the company hopes to achieve through its business.

Once the company's long-term vision is established, all strategy can be developed and linked to that vision: operations, finance, sales, human resources and research and development. The more time a company takes to crystallize its vision and develop strategies around it, the greater the synergy it will experience in accomplishing that vision. Maintaining a focus on the company's longer-term vision and goals should also weigh heavily on the outcome of short-term decisions.

Values

Values set the tone for how people work together. They form the primary expectation for behavior and work-related outcomes. With flatter organizational structures, employees are being given much more autonomy now than at any time in the past, especially in small to mid-sized organizations. Values that are ingrained into the corporate culture provide a compass for employees to align their actions against. If employees embrace the same set of core values, then it's easier to delegate tasks knowing that the person performing the work is aware of the expectations.

For values to be effective in influencing corporate culture, they need to form the foundation for all relationships within the organization, including how employees are hired and how success is evaluated. Values must be modeled by leaders and be demonstrated through the daily behavior of everyone who works for the company.

The process of establishing corporate values should include as many of the company's employees as possible through discussion, focus groups or surveys. The goal is to determine the primary shared values that will help you achieve your vision. It begins by asking questions and analyzing feedback to determine what motivates your employees to do an excellent job, rather than just completing their assigned tasks. Some of the values that emerge may include: integrity, respect for others, teamwork, quality, communication excellence, focus on results, embracing change, trust and innovation. Every company's set of values is distinctly theirs, based on what they value in the workplace and in life.

Communication

Communication is a company's tool for expressing its values, vision and expectations. If the message is clear and consistently expresses the same goal in all aspects of the business, the result will be the trust and commitment of employees.

For communication to be effective, employees and leaders at all levels need to be comfortable communicating expectations, soliciting input and feedback, and engaging in ongoing dialogue regarding business processes, decisions, priorities and successes. One of the tools we introduce to organizations is the development of a set of organization-wide expectations that mirror its vision and values. In the absence of job descriptions or formal written processes, these expectation statements act as guidelines regarding performance and meeting customer needs. The expectations are not developed to force conformity; they are about giving people a framework within which to use their own creativity, skills and passion to help the company achieve its vision.

As a leader, do you provide performance-related feedback only once a year or not at all? If so, then you are making your life more difficult than it needs to be. Feedback and discussions about an employee's performance are the most underutilized communication and team-building tools available to managers. Take the time to develop your own format for providing feedback based on an employee's ability to demonstrate your values and expectations on a consistent basis. For some companies, quarterly or monthly one-on-one sessions between employee and manager are the most effective format. For others, they may feel more comfortable developing a written document. Each company is unique and needs to tap its own creativity to develop a process that all managers will support and actually use to strengthen internal communication and foster more open and honest dialogue.

Trust

Running a business requires the skill and dedication of a large number of people with diverse skill sets. If you have hired the right people, they need to have full accountability and authority to act within their position. You need to trust that they will know what to do and how to do it, and that they will make decisions based on the company's vision and values. If you do not trust your managers or employees, or if you doubt their skills, you need to find others you can depend upon. Without absolute trust in your team's commitment and skills, you will be compensating for their weaknesses and negatively impacting other areas of your business.

Truth is the other side of trust. In an authentic workplace, being truthful in communication and interaction with all employees, customers and suppliers is the way things are done—no exceptions! In most employer-employee relationships, we don't want to hurt others' feelings, so we tell half-truths in hopes that others will pick up on our hints about how to change. People may feel more comfortable avoiding confrontation, but by not addressing issues head-on and being truthful about expectations, the situation will fester. Inaction and avoidance will not help the problem go away. How do you begin to increase your honesty? Let your actions speak for themselves. Approach every work situation with integrity, be known for providing your honest opinion, and take responsibility for your action, even in times of failure or disappointment. Should the time come that you have to address performance issues or deliver bad news, your colleagues and employees will respect you, based on the trust and integrity you have demonstrated on a daily basis.

2. People

The unique element in each organization that can drive long-term competitive advantage is its people, their skills and their motivation. People may play different roles within an organization, but they all have the same desire to feel connected to the company and to have an impact through their work. If a company selects employees who can complement the rhythm of the business, share the corporate values and understand the vision, it will create greater synergies and more focused results.

Even the most talented people can see their productivity drop when their experiences in the workplace fail to live up to their expectations. Bright, talented and highly motivated people take a proactive approach to their careers and are not sitting around waiting for their next opportunity. Once they become disenchanted with their job or the company, they seek out another opportunity to awaken their souls and meet their career development needs. In building a strong company, the key for an employer is to create a work environment and corporate culture that engages talented individuals, maintains their interest and encourages them to follow their passion within the organization.

How can you get creative to keep more of the right people and help more of the wrong people self-select out? The stronger your corporate culture and the consistency of your vision, values and focus, the easier it is for people to understand if the workplace is a fit for them. The goal is to attract and retain a motivated, highly skilled workforce. When you use values as criteria in the hiring process and actively manage performance expectations, those who do not fit are more easily identified and will often leave when required to demonstrate performance.

Employees

Have you ever listened to someone describe their job and the company they work for with such enthusiasm that you thought, "I'd like to work for that company too"? When you love your job, are challenged by the opportunities and connect with the company's product and vision, you can't help but become an ambassador for your organization whenever you talk about your work.

Within the next five to ten years, there will be more people retiring from the workforce than young people entering it. While the shrinking workforce will make qualified candidates harder to find, it does not mean that a company can drop its hiring standards. Hiring the right people who fit with an organization's culture and values requires a focused and consistent approach to recruitment. An authentic workplace priority in hiring needs to be based on behavioral interviewing techniques that assess individuals against the company's values. As a leader, you need to devote resources to teach managers and others involved in the hiring process how to select candidates based on your corporate values and workplace expectations, in addition to technical skill requirements. Apply those same values and expectations you hire for to the methods you use to review, reward and compensate employees. This will dovetail the human resource strategy to support the corporate vision.

It is not realistic to have only the best and brightest employees from your industry working for you. Every company is a blend of high achievers, solid performers, junior-level contributors and some who can contribute effectively but only in limited knowledge areas. Your goal in the hiring process is to continually increase your talent roster to give you additional capability and depth to succeed in your target market and to potentially surpass your business objectives. In addition to advancing your talent capabilities through recruitment, you also need to invest in existing employees to build their problem-solving, communication and leadership abilities so they can continue to contribute effectively over the longer term.

If an employee struggles with weaknesses in non-core aspects of their job, it may be easier to work to their strengths; however, don't just ignore their weaknesses. Provide training, coaching and mentorship to mitigate the impact of weakness on corporate results. Managers must be prepared to address performance issues as they arise. Weaknesses should not be ignored, as they can create a drag on your company's performance as others compensate and make up the slack.

Leaders

A position title does not necessarily equate to leadership abilities. Business leaders come from a multitude of backgrounds with varying levels of education and experience. Strategically focused companies not only recognize this, but also actively develop leaders and leadership abilities within every level of the organization to ensure adequate skill depth and succession potential. There are, unfortunately, many organizations that will promote individuals into senior levels without the required skills and an understanding of the role a leader is required to play. You will recognize these managers. They tend to be more concerned about themselves and the needs of their department than they are about contributing to the achievement of goals and forward movement of the overall corporate plan.

But what sets good leaders apart? It can depend on the culture or environment of the organization, but there are some telltale signs we observe through our work. Less effective managers see their role as more of a supervisor: maintaining the status quo, making top-down decisions, relying on long-standing procedures, overseeing or micromanaging work. While this is a safe method of managing in more junior roles, these managers need to develop a different mindset to be successful at higher levels and in true leadership positions.

Successful leaders view their role differently. As the leader, their goal is to influence change and improve the effectiveness of their department or team. They do this through more collaborative decision making, coaching their staff to be problem solvers, and managing timelines and outcomes of work rather than focusing on detailed work methods. Their employees have the tools, skills and training to do their jobs and fully understand the accountability and expectations of their position. The other quality we observe in this more successful group of leaders is their ability to think longer term about how their department will actively contribute to the goals of the company. In addition to managing the day-to-day activities of their team, a portion of their time is devoted to increasing efficiencies, developing the skill base of their employees and proactively collaborating with other departments to improve communication and processes.

Today, leaders need to be coaches, mentors, facilitators, negotiators, innovators and problem solvers. The type of leader working within any given organization is a factor of the corporate culture, recruitment effectiveness, workplace expectations, executive coaching and performance management. The executive team must "walk the talk" and actively model, reinforce and reward the leadership style and performance expectations they support. If they can't support an organization's culture and values, they are pulling others down with them and it may be time to reconsider their employment.

Developing an Authentic Workplace

To transform your workplace into an authentic one, you need a leadership team committed to living the company's vision and values and championing them internally throughout the organization and in all external relationships. With the right people in place, take the time to develop a strategy for change—a long-term plan to shift your culture and realign organizational practices to support the vision.

It all starts with the leadership team, whose responsibility it is to effectively steward and manage people, processes, resources and relationships to add value to the organization. This group of individuals must fully embrace the company's vision and values and understand the importance of using them as the foundation for all business practices and communication. Their role is to become active and visible champions dedicated to challenging the status quo to ensure business is conducted in a manner that is authentic to the corporate vision.

With the right team in place, you can begin to plan your strategy for change. This is not a six-month or year-long process you are undertaking; your task is to begin reviewing how you conduct your business from the ground up and to realign priorities and expectations. The following ABC strategies will be helpful.

A. Use the vision-values test

For every new policy, procedure, practice, system and guideline you implement throughout the organization, ask the following questions:

- How does it support the corporate vision?
- Will it move us closer to our goal or potentially hinder our progress?
- Is it congruent with our values?
- Is this a short-term, reactionary solution or will this still make sense three years from now?

B. Audit your practices

How can you prepare for change if you are not aware of how your current business methods either support or block progression toward your corporate vision or run counter to your values? Evaluate your business systems and practices through one or more of the following processes to assess strengths and gaps between your current practices and what you need to become more authentic:

- Commit to an employee survey;
- Audit your operations, sales and human resources practices;
- Conduct a 360-degree leadership assessment.

C. Create an implementation plan

Becoming authentic is not an event but, rather, a journey of creating greater clarity about your corporate vision and how it is reflected in your business practices. Plan to undertake one or two initiatives a year that will strengthen your corporate strategy and business skill depth, such as:

- Developing a stronger leadership team;
- Increasing communication and the flow of information across the organization;
- Implementing a values-based approach to the recruitment and retention of staff;
- Creating a customer feedback process.

Introduce a New Rhythm and Tempo

Authenticity is about becoming transparent to your employees, your stakeholders and your customers. It is about truly living your corporate vision in all aspects of the business through telling the truth, building business capabilities and delivering the best possible product to your customer by engaging your employees in your vision.

Employees aren't just asking for congruency between corporate vision and the way you do business, they are demanding it. They no longer tolerate inaction and conflicting values. Instead, they are leaving those types of organizations to find a company that connects with their passion and personal values. Do not walk away from this book and do nothing. In six months or three years, you may still be frustrated and looking for answers. Regardless of the type of company you work in, how long you've been in business and who your clients are, the following are 10 steps you can take today to better engage your employees in realizing your corporate vision.

1. Hire people who share your values and connect with your vision. No one area impacts organizational performance and culture as greatly as the hiring process. Get it right and your competitive advantage and productivity will soar. Get it wrong and you will spend most of your time in crisis management mode.

2. Teach employees about your business so they can fully contribute. Nothing frustrates an employee more than wanting to add value in their role but having their knowledge restricted to their own department. Introduce new employees to your company's executives and thought leaders during your orientation process to facilitate their access to information and resources.

3. Create and support a problem-solving culture. Challenge employees at all levels of the organization to think like a leader and be prepared to present solutions along with problems. If they know your vision, employee suggestions will have a greater likelihood of being relevant to your corporate goals.

4. Challenge people to think long-term in their decisions. The resolution of a problem and the speed of the decision are not as important as the type of solution. Make sure it supports your long-term vision and goals rather than creating a short-term solution.

5. Give honest, open and frequent feedback. Build regular performance-related discussions into monthly employee one-on-ones. And while you're at it, ask employees for their candid feedback on your management style. Communication is a two-way street.

6. Differentiate between your high- and low-potential employees. Let those who perform at the highest levels of competency, efficiency and productivity know how valued they are, and reward them accordingly through a re-earnable bonus or other monetary and non-monetary means.

7. Engage your clients in regular feedback and improvement forums. Don't ignore your revenue stream as a source of feedback to strengthen your business strategy. Your best customers will be more than happy to provide the feedback, especially if it adds value to your business relationship. But be prepared to address their feedback.

8. Live your values in all business systems. From sales to finance, and operations to human resources, review your policies and priorities to ensure they align with your articulated values.

9. Let your managers manage. Management is about actively managing people and expectations. When expectations are clear and an employee fails to meet your standards, the manager's job is to address the issue in a timely fashion. Now is not the time to develop a new policy or procedure to make up for the inaction of a few who like to challenge expectations. These reactionary policies only serve to restrict the guidelines followed by the majority of employees without incident.

10. Be prepared to feel uncomfortable and address "elephants" in the room.
Proactively address conflict as it occurs. It generally doesn't go away but, instead, festers and evolves into more numerous tensions or becomes ambiguous and more difficult to address.

There is no single type of authentic workplace. Whether your business is retail, technical, manufacturing or a business service, you can celebrate your unique vision and engage the passion of your employees toward your vision. Companies have the best chance of attracting and retaining top talent by creating and nurturing authentic workplaces. Through the focused application of the corporate vision and values throughout the organization, companies can awaken the spirits and talents of their best and brightest employees to create the synergies for success.

Because no two workplaces are the same, you need to invest time and effort into developing the business practices and corporate culture that will support your vision. If you can create congruity between your vision, your external brand and internal practices, you will experience a dramatic increase in your business results.

Audrey Ciccone

Audrey Ciccone is focused on building business success by developing long-term strategies that reflect her clients' entrepreneurial spirit and unique corporate vision. Her company, Human Perspective Consulting Ltd., specializes in working at the executive level with small to medium-sized companies who compete globally in their niche markets.

Audrey's passion is reading the pulse of a business to create more authentic workplaces where employees connect with the organization's vision and values. She approaches corporate performance and profitability from a human perspective based on private sector experience conducting organizational analysis, due diligence, system audits, program design and implementation. She is a trusted business advisor developing long-term client relationships focused on connecting corporate vision with process, policy and results.

Audrey has a degree in Psychology from the University of British Columbia and is a Certified Human Resource Professional (CHRP). Audrey serves on the board of directors for the Business Information Technology Network (BitNet) and is a past board member of the Fraser Valley Technology Network in Vancouver, BC.

Business Name:	Human Perspective Consulting Ltd.
Address:	2910 South Sheridan Way, Oakville, ON L6J 7L9
Telephone:	905-699-7721
Fax:	905-842-7102
E-mail:	aciccone@human-perspective.com
Web Address:	www.human-perspective.com
Professional Affiliations:	Canadian Association of Professional Speakers (CAPS), Human Resources Professionals Association of Ontario (HRPAO)

Favorite Quote:

Leadership is lifting a person's vision to higher sights, the raising of a person's performance to a higher standard, the building of a personality beyond its normal limitations.

—Peter F. Drucker

Sharon Bar-David

Sharon Bar-David Speaking and Training

Let Change Become You:
Boosting Your Change Resilience

Since change has become an integral part of today's workplace, common sense would dictate that most of us are able to readily accept it, embrace it, perhaps even celebrate it. In reality, my work with hundreds of organizations indicates that the exact opposite is true: the overwhelming majority of people have developed an allergy-like reaction to workplace change. They experience it as upsetting and disruptive. It interferes with their need for stability. Change is demanding, exhausting and unwanted.

If you are one of these people, this chapter is for you. The good news is this: You have the capacity to boost your change resilience. Once you set your mind to doing so and once you acquire the right tools, you'll find yourself facing any type of workplace change with more ease and flexibility. In the following pages, you will find valuable information about the most common change-related errors people make and learn powerful strategies for increasing your overall change resilience.

When It Comes to Change, Size Doesn't Matter!

It is widely accepted that large-scale organizational change will invariably have an impact on people. We tend to think of mergers, acquisitions, downsizing, restructuring, and the like, as classic triggers for negative reactions. Smaller changes, which may not even register as "change" from management's perspective, are often overlooked. Yet, these seemingly small changes can have a profound effect on people's resilience. A participant in one of my sessions once talked about the detrimental effect that the move from one office space to another, just ten feet away, had had on her; she called it her "real estate changes." She described how in her first office, if she stretched her neck upward to its maximum limit and then tilted it exactly 45 degrees sideways and 10 degrees forward, she could catch a glimpse of Lake Ontario. Upon seeing the lake, an immediate sense of well-being would descend upon her. Her new office, though boasting a larger window, looked over an unattractive city view. She now had nowhere to turn to for her cherished sense of calm.

The magnitude of the change has little correlation with its actual impact on individual people. A seemingly small "real estate change" can have as large an impact as any mega change.

The Shift

Resilience to change requires that you shift from a *reactive* position to a *proactive* and *responsive* one. As the diagram below illustrates, most people react to change by falling into predictable traps. Knowing what these traps are is the first step to replacing old reactive habits with a more resilient response.

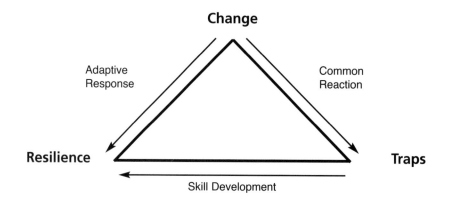

If you are a mid-level manager or senior executive and think that you don't need to read this chapter, think again. Different organizational levels are prone to different traps. Your own actions may have inadvertently contributed to the erosion of people's resilience and exacerbated their "allergic" reactions. Productivity, engagement and trust may have been impacted.

Not long ago, I was called to consult to the CEO of a mid-size Canadian company regarding the matter of resilience in his organization. Here is what transpired:

>> The CEO's concern was that two divisions within the company suffered from low morale, reduced engagement and incessant complaining. Through my probing, it was revealed that some 14 months earlier the company had decided to do some cost cutting and streamlining. They let go of a division leader and eliminated the position altogether. This man was revered by his group and was a high performer. What the senior leadership did not appreciate until our meeting was the extent to which this move would affect people's resilience and how this eroded resilience would impact the business itself. As the CEO put it, "I wish we had had this conversation 16 months ago!" Within two months, a new division head was hired and many of the problems subsided. <<

From Control to Influence

Developing change resilience entails a shift from the notion of *control* to the notion of *influence*. We tend to fall into the trap of believing that there's little we can do to control the way things are going. As our sense of control slips away, we start thinking and behaving in non-productive, self-defeating ways.

Once you shift to a focus on influence rather than on control, you might realize that within the change, there are numerous things you can impact. It may be in the form of constructive suggestions as to how things could be done better, or perhaps it is deciding to positively influence the atmosphere within your team.

Developing change resilience begins with changing the way you think. Once your thinking changes, your behavior will follow. One of the most beneficial

adjustments you can make is to train yourself to be influence focused. You'll be amazed at the results!

The Common Reaction: Falling Into Traps

Human beings are funny creatures—we fall into different thinking and behavioral errors that limit our ability to face new challenges constructively. In my training and coaching work with thousands of people in a variety of industries, I've observed people at all levels fall time and again into predictable traps. It is imperative to understand what these traps are; if you do not know where your soft spots reside, you won't be able to change-proof yourself effectively.

The traps we fall into when we encounter change are frighteningly similar to the bear traps used by Northern Ontario authorities. These are 40-inch by 40-inch by 8-foot cages with see-through mesh walls, mounted on a trailer. A chunk of bait at the far end of the cage lures the bear to enter. Once it enters, the door shuts, locked, behind it. The cage can now be hitched onto another vehicle and the bear is transported to a safer habitat in the wilderness. The bear can sit, lie down or stand inside the cage quite comfortably, but its freedom to act is limited to the cage's confines. Anything outside the cage's perimeters is inaccessible. The bear is no longer free.

When we get stuck in a rigid way of viewing a specific change, we are just as trapped as the bear. We seemingly keep moving, doing, talking and performing, but it's all within a very limited perimeter. Our options are reduced only to those available within our limited perception of reality.

Being human means that we are bound to get trapped on occasion. Being resilient means that we are able to detect our difficulty early on and free ourselves quickly. Each organizational level is vulnerable to its own set of traps. Most notable are:

Senior Leaders	➡	The Optical Trap
Middle Management	➡	The Sandwich Trap
Employees	➡	The Quicksand Trap

Senior Leaders: The Optical Trap

The role of senior leadership is to see the big picture. Top leaders focus on the forest, not the trees. Their duty is to look ahead in a visionary manner and lead the organization forward.

This very orientation to future and to vision makes leaders vulnerable to the Optical Trap. As a leader, once you have taken care of the big-picture part of the change, your focus shifts to the next necessary change. As you do so, your optical field automatically narrows. You are unable to see that the people below you are still struggling with implementing the frustrating, infinite details of the change.

Another key element of the Optical Trap is this: while you had long ago come to terms with the old ways having ended, the people below you are still mourning. They may be experiencing a sense of loss over the "real estate changes" or over a departed colleague or manager, or a system that they had previously mastered.

When those below you try expressing the sense of loss or pointing to genuine problems with the new way, you might fall into yet another trap: you may get impatient with their "whining," lack of buy-in and tumbling performance.

A negative push-pull cycle will now commence: your concern that people are too past-obsessed will lead you to increasingly focus your communication on the compelling future. You might intensify your efforts to emphasize the need to embrace the new way and to move forward with gusto and commitment. Beware of this trap, as you will create the very opposite effect of what you are hoping to achieve: the more you push forward, the more people will pull back. Your actions will inadvertently cause employees to fall into their own set of traps; negativity, victimhood and mistrust will grow exponentially.

Middle Management: The Sandwich Trap

As a mid-level manager, you are "sandwiched" between senior management and front-line employees. This inevitably puts you in a highly stressful position and renders you vulnerable to a specific set of traps.

The biggest trap that you might fall into is *either-or thinking*. This means you tend to think in extremes, with very little middle ground. For example, you might fear that speaking honestly about your own struggles or reservations means that you're not doing your job or that you're not a team player. Or you may think that, "If I let my people talk too much about the negative, they'll never be able to look at the positive" or "If I let this kind of talk go on, no work will ever get done around here."

Paradoxically, the exact opposite is true: once you liberate yourself from the *either-or* framework, you are freed to become an authentic, transparent leader. You can express your own feelings about the change while also leading forward decisively. You can let people air their feelings. In fact, the more you let that happen, the more they will feel heard. As they feel understood, trust will increase, and with it, the capacity to move forward.

Employees: The Quicksand Trap

The single most common trap into which employees fall is *negativity*. Its symptoms include resistance, complaining, doubting management's agenda and integrity, engaging in rumors, bitterness, low morale, displays of anger and low motivation. Like quicksand, once you allow negativity to become a part of your way of thinking, it turns into a trap from which escape is difficult or impossible. Negativity is extremely contagious and its symptoms spread very quickly. Whenever I ask an audience, "How many of you have fallen into the trap of negativity at least once?" 100 percent of participants raise their hand! Furthermore, the question always brings about lots of laughter and comments, along the lines of "Only once? How about five times *today*?"

Related traps that you, as an employee, might fall into are *victimhood*, *cynicism*, and *mistrust*. And finally, you might fall into the trap of *disengagement*. Under the influence of this trap, you might stop caring about the organization altogether. When disengaged, you will have stripped your relationship with the organization to the bare bones of the employment contract, in other words, "I'll do the minimum necessary in exchange for a defined amount of money and benefits." The impact on you is that vitality and creativity subside and work becomes a fatiguing chore.

The Adaptive Response: Change Resilience

Becoming resilient is an adaptive and creative response to the challenge of change. Rather than reacting to change, we need to develop a more adaptive response. There are two types of adaptive responses that I've identified as 1) Proactive Resilience, and 2) Real-time Resilience. Proactive Resilience encompasses all the things one needs to do in anticipation of any type of change that might occur. Real-time Resilience involves all actions you take to respond effectively to a specific change as it unfolds. We'll look further at these types of resilience and then outline practical ways for practicing them.

Proactive Resilience

Before a flight takes off, much effort is put into ensuring that the aircraft and its crew are equipped to deal with any possible challenges. The plane's airworthiness is checked frequently. The pilot's competence is routinely examined. The airline and aviation authorities require that he pass grueling simulator challenges. Pre-departure, the pilot pores over extensive checklists to ensure that everything is in place to guarantee a safe flight. Pilot and airline both prepare for any type of known or unknown risk the flight might encounter.

> **Being change resilient requires that you prepare for change in exactly the same way that the pilot prepares to fly. There are things you can do to increase your change resilience long before you encounter a specific change. These preparatory actions, practices and thought patterns are known as *Proactive Resilience*.**

Proactive Resilience helps mitigate our tendency to experience workplace change as surprising or unexpected. Once you experience change as a blow of sorts, you are likely to react to it rather than respond. In fact, your body will kick in its innate fight-or-flight response. When this response is activated, a series of profound changes occur in the body and mind. Adrenaline and cortisol gush through the system and you are primed to experience any demand on you as endangering your very existence.

Proactive Resilience ensures that regardless of the type or scope of change you encounter, you will be ready to meet it with flexibility and pliability. When it is not possible for a plane to land at its original destination due to bad weather, its backup systems, extra fuel and pilot's pre-flight acquaintance with alternate landing sites, all will ensure that the plane can still land successfully.

You, too, have the obligation to prepare in such a way that no matter what change you face, you land safely. Cultivating your Proactive Resilience will give you that calm, reassuring feeling of "I can handle any change that might come my way." It will build your confidence. This state of confidence will guarantee that your body keeps the levels of adrenaline and cortisol under check. In turn, when you encounter change, your system will respond with resourcefulness and flexibility.

Take the case of Tom, a plant manager for one of Canada's most respected companies. When consulting to Tom and assisting the plant's employees through a massive change initiative, I came to appreciate him as a leader at the top of his game. He led the change initiative decisively and demonstrated strong people skills. Several months after the change was successfully implemented, with extremely high levels of employee support, Tom was let go. You might think that Tom was devastated and angry. In fact, he was not. As it turns out, the shock of termination was cushioned by several key strategies Tom had employed in advance to change-proof himself. Stay tuned, as some of these strategies will be described below.

Strategies for Expanding Your Proactive Resilience

1. Foster "healthy paranoia." A pilot and crew are required to relentlessly scan the environment in search of any risk that might remotely threaten the smooth progression of the flight. In the same vein, a certain amount of suspicion and worry in the workplace is a healthy thing. Do not allow yourself to be lulled into thinking that things will always be the same or that your position is secure because you happen to be a high performer or a long-time employee. If your gut tells you that you might be at risk, follow up and check it out!

In Tom's case, long before he was let go, he began sensing that his direct manager was not fully appreciative of him. Even though the change initiative was going very well, and despite accolades from plant employees and from other parts of the organization, his own boss did not seem as enthused as would be expected. Rather than ignoring his observations, Tom began mentally preparing for the fact that he might not last long in his position. He did not tell himself that this was not fair, nor did he say that the project's success would speak for itself. Rather, it was a matter of reading the map with a cold, assessing eye and accepting reality for what it was.

2. Develop strong skills and a ready-to-go resume. There's nothing like an updated set of skills and a polished resume to make you feel that no matter what comes your way, your parachute is ready.

Proactive Resilience requires that you continuously expand your skills. Make sure to update your written resume every three to six months with the new skills you've acquired. Doing so will remind you of your worth and build your confidence. The more confident you are, the less threatening change will be. Furthermore, the more skilled you are, the stronger your position within the organization.

Let's return to Tom's story: Four years before I met him, Tom had enrolled in a nighttime MBA program. He had decided to enhance his own marketability and knowledge, even though a graduate degree was not essential to advancement in his line of work. Going back to school was a significant challenge: he was a family man and the plant required long hours. The program was six years' long, but Tom persisted. When he was let go, he was close to completing the program. He dedicated several months to full-time studies, graduated successfully, and...stay tuned for what happened next!

3. Develop a broad network. In situations where change has had a significantly negative impact, someone's outreached hand can save the day. Thus, a strong network is crucial. Such a network should include people both within your organization and outside it. Within, make sure you develop relationships with people from other departments and levels. Outside the organization, maintain contact and support with people in your current industry and in related industries. In both cases, learn about what's going on in the field and seek ways to be helpful to these people. Make sure they know exactly what you do and familiarize them with your strengths.

And Tom? During the months following his termination, Tom began going to meetings over coffee with lots of people he knew from his past, even if only loosely. Once he graduated, an opportunity emerged as a result of a connection made in one of these meetings. Tom was hired for a new job, very different from his old one, where he was able to use his new skills and expertise.

4. Become your own coach. Sometimes, we get complacent. We neglect to realize that just like any other entity within the marketplace, we need to ensure that our little unit can thrive under any market conditions.

Appoint yourself as your own business coach. As coach, invite yourself to deal head-on with the following challenges: Do you convey the right "brand," or image, to the world? Is your "customer service" (as practiced with colleagues, real customers and managers) responsive and reliable? Are you familiar with the latest developments in your field and aware of trends that might affect you? What "marketing" efforts are you engaged in? Do enough people know what you offer and how you are different from the next person? Are you working diligently to assess the risks that might affect you?

5. Adopt ongoing stress-busting practices. Change and stress go hand in hand. By building stress-busting practices into your daily life, you will increase the chances that when change takes place, your system will retain more of its equilibrium. Simple things such as sufficient sleep, healthy eating, exercise, yoga, meditation, prayer, mindfulness, counting your blessing, hobbies, prioritizing, saying "no" and delegating will go a long way in reducing your overall stress and making you more change ready.

Real-time Resilience

Your workplace change resilience will be put to the test when you are presented with a real-life change situation. Here is where you will be prone to falling into the various traps. You might find it difficult to bounce back or to keep a positive focus. Or you might feel tempted to act like a victim rather than as a powerful individual.

Real-time Resilience is comprised of the actions you take in response to a specific change situation. It's what enables you to rise to the occasion and respond to the change constructively. Real-time Resilience is akin to the actions that pilot and crew take to handle a specific threat as it unfolds.

In order to develop a robust change-resilience practice, it is crucial to develop both Proactive and Real-time Resilience. They are interdependent and interrelated. If you practice Proactive Resilience on a regular basis, Real-time Resilience becomes much easier to apply. In fact, you might find that Real-time Resilience seems like an extension of what you have already been doing. You will not need to reinvent the wheel or familiarize yourself with new strategies at a time when you need to preserve precious energy for dealing with the real situation at hand.

Strategies for Boosting Your Real-time Resilience

Real-time Resilience requires you to gain tight control of any thought patterns that might hinder your ability to respond to the change with maximum agility. If you do not control such thoughts, your behavior will invariably become self-destructive. Within the confines of this short chapter, I will highlight only a handful of strategies, clustered under two categories: 1) managing your mind, and 2) influencing your environment.

1. Managing your mind: During times of change, your own mind can become your worst enemy. It is crucial to set aside the tendency to think about the change in catastrophizing ways. Instead, every effort needs to be made to think of the change in realistic terms. Furthermore, instead of spending precious energy on things that are not going the way you want them to, keep a steady focus on the things over which you *do* have control or influence. First and foremost, you always *do* have control over your own attitude, no matter how difficult the circumstances might be!

Organizational change always presents valuable opportunities for growth, advancement and relationship building. These opportunities will reveal themselves if you keep an open eye. Actively uncover and seize these opportunities. If you do so, new paths will open for you, either within your current organization or elsewhere.

2. Influencing your environment: As part of enhancing your Real-time Resilience, learn to express your needs and ideas in a constructive fashion. Many participants in my sessions have told me that during change, free expression seems too risky. The key is not *what* you say but *how* you say it. If you articulate only the negative or come across as whiny, people won't hear you. You will be perceived as a non-contributor with all the implications of this label. Deliver your message at the right time and place and with the right tone. And always accompany any critique with suggested solutions!

Use the change to get noticed. During change, there are ample opportunities to showcase your skills, strengths and positive attitude. A positive, "can do" attitude will particularly stand out against the backdrop of negativity and disengagement. Once you are noticed—especially by higher-ups—exciting opportunities within the change are likely to come your way.

I recall a time when I was a front-line employee in an organization going through major changes, complete with a new CEO. Within two weeks of the CEO's arrival, I sent him a personal e-mail, lamenting the lack of adornments in the corridors and public spaces. I suggested eight zero-cost ideas for changing this, including ideas for using the walls to celebrate the multi-cultural nature of the organization. Within two hours, I received a personal e-mail from him, and by the next day, we met in his office to discuss my ideas.

Most importantly, become magnetic. Choose to become a point of positive energy in the midst of the negativity surrounding you. Contribute generously of your ideas and vitality. Support others. You will draw similar energy towards you. Before long, your whole experience of the changes will shift.

Leaders' Perspectives on Proactive and Real-time Resilience

As a leader, you must first ensure that your own resilience is well-developed. Without it, the ongoing vibrations, shudders, shifts and quakes of change will strip you of everything you have going for you. Furthermore, your people will look to you for inspiration, and if your resilience is not authentic, your public face will quickly crack.

For people in leadership positions, resilience is comprised of two complementary components: personal resilience and resilience-oriented leadership. The personal resilience strategies discussed in the previous pages apply to you in exactly the same way that they apply to front-line employees.

In addition, it is crucial that you create a change-resilient work environment for your people. A resilience-oriented leadership style will prove priceless when your people have to deal with actual change. Rather than suffering from negativity and declining performance, they will be able to focus on the change in a productive way.

Place resilience firmly within your optical field at all times. As you plan any change, crucial questions need to be asked: What do we need to do in order to protect people's resilience? What, when and how do we need to communicate in order to mitigate people's tendency to fall into traps? How can we maintain trust levels during times of change? How do we honor feelings of loss, while simultaneously keeping a focus on the target?

I've seen too many organizations where leaders have the right intentions but do not ask the right questions. Like the CEO who let go of the division head, they are later surprised at the results of their actions. It is so much easier to plan correctly in advance than to fix things in hindsight.

A Closing Invitation

In today's corporate world, if you do not manage change, *it* will manage *you*. It is crucial that you learn to identify the traps into which you might fall. Once you do that, make sure to nurture your Proactive Resilience on an ongoing basis. And when a specific change comes knocking, consciously work on boosting your Real-time Resilience.

Here's my invitation to you: take action today to change-proof yourself. Furthermore, turn yourself into a positive force that impacts on those around you. It will make a world of difference. Let change become you!

Sharon Bar-David

Sharon Bar-David helps people at all organizational levels boost their resilience. Hundreds of organizations have leveraged her expertise through the keynote speeches, seminars and coaching she offers. Sharon helps her clients strengthen personal and professional performance in the areas of change, stress, communication, conflict and work-life harmony.

Sharon's clients benefit from the insights she gained in more than 20 years' experience as lawyer, trainer, speaker, consultant and family therapist. She has worked extensively with North American and Middle-East organizations within a wide range of industries. She has gained an outstanding reputation for her clear and persuasive messages and for a style that is motivational, informative and highly entertaining.

After launching her career as a litigation lawyer, Sharon immigrated to Canada and pursued a Masters of Social Work degree, followed by a post-graduate fellowship in Family Systems Therapy. Before long, she discovered that her real mission was to make this world a better place, one group at a time. She launched a career in speaking and training and has been joyfully at it since 1991.

Business Name:	Sharon Bar-David Speaking and Training
Address:	49 Fairleigh Crescent, Toronto, ON M6C 3S1
Telephone:	416-781-8132
E-mail:	sbd@sharonbardavid.com
Web Address:	www.sharonbardavid.com
Professional Affiliations:	Canadian Association of Professional Speakers; International Federation of Professional Speakers; Ontario Association of Social Workers

Beverly Beuermann-King

Work Smart Live Smart, R 'n' B Consulting

You Need a Strong Wheel on a Bumpy Road

Doing more with less. Downsizing. Evolving technology. Productivity gains. ROI. With all of the fast-paced demands and bumps along the corporate road, today's leaders need to manage their own stress and assist their teams to identify and implement strategies that will reduce or eliminate the *impact* of their stress as well. The expectation is growing for leaders to be accountable for overall physical, social and mental well-being—while keeping productivity and profitability high.

In order to be successful, today's leaders need to understand the implications of organizational wellness, their role in its development and the strategies that can get them there. Very few companies are providing this leadership training to their front-line or senior managers. With the exploding rate of employees on stress leave and utilizing prescription drugs, along with the resulting cost to companies, this training is essential.

Organizational health can boost your bottom line.

Successful leaders know that their people are the most important resource that their organization has and that healthy employees are the only way to achieve business success. Studies continue to prove this interconnected relationship between the bottom line, healthy employees and leadership support.

As the leader, you continually hear the words "support," "trust," "respect," "flexibility" and "inclusion." Yet, you are not provided the context or tools necessary to successfully implement strategies that result in improved organizational health. By incorporating our simple SOS approach and applying it to the key areas of your business, you will be able to develop a workplace that is supportive, engaged and competitive, and one that inspires your employees to choose a healthy and active lifestyle.

Supportive leaders take action.

An insightful leader gets great results. The following example provides a snapshot of this:

>> Jim, a young man in his thirties, is a talented, creative employee who excels at project management. His boss presented him with the challenge to develop a new line of consumer products. Jim was informed of the "big picture" so he could see how these new products fit in with the whole organization's mission. Goals were set and he clearly knew what direction to head and what standards he was being measured against. Jim's talents in planning, organizing and project management were fully utilized. The company supported him in taking courses and training to ensure that this developmental process was effective and efficient. His boss monitored his progress and inquired about the personal and familial impact of this project for Jim. And when the project was completed, Jim was publicly recognized for the success of the new product line. <<

As a caring leader, it is critical to know what is important to support, engage and retain your employees. Jim's example and current research show that your employees want:

- respect and appreciation;
- to know what is expected from them;
- the necessary resources to do their job;
- to be able to use their talents;
- the freedom to speak up and to feel heard;
- to work in an environment free from threats;
- to belong and to have support;

- periods of calm and stress relief.

There is no magic key to success. When you see employee wellness as an important investment, you are able to match many effective strategies to produce healthy, engaged teams. You will realize a greater bottom-line success than your competitors who don't.

Employees leave a boss—not a job.

Reality is that many employees who move on don't leave because of their job. They leave because of their boss:

> » The day came when Jim's boss moved on, as is the case in other real life companies today. Enter the new boss who was controlling, demanding and short-sighted. Things changed quickly and dramatically. Jim was not given the full picture; in fact, he was told that the big picture was none of his concern. He was not given positive feedback; in fact, he was given no feedback at all. Jim was not recognized for his continued efforts to succeed and improve the product. Trust waned, enthusiasm died, and commitment ceased in this toxic workplace. Finally, Jim left. After eight years, the organization lost an exceptional employee «

You have probably seen how one bad leader can have a far-reaching and negative impact on the corporate bottom line through products that are poorly made, in poor customer service and in a lack of problem-solving ability. Poor leadership can kill creativity, cause problems, and produce a wide variety of negative physical and mental outcomes within their team. It can become a very bumpy ride for all.

SOS for Leaders

As a leader, where do you start? Too often leaders bounce from one "emergency" to another or from one hot topic or flavor-of-the-month to another. This piecemeal approach to leadership and assisting your team leaves you tired out, maxed out and often feeling hopeless as your overall impact is minimized. The easiest way for you to implement the right strategies at the right time and to have a clear picture of how to break it all down is to focus on a holistic SOS approach to organizational and employee health:

S	➡	Situation
O	➡	Ourselves
S	➡	Support

In this model, the first "S" stands for addressing the **Situation**. These are the situations, challenges and issues that your team is facing. These include the culture in which employees are trying to cope, the environment in which they work and the issues and circumstances they are facing. It means communicating clear goals, direction and connection to the mission and vision of the company. It means supplying the resources to allow your team to do their job the right way and getting rid of outdated machines, policies and procedures that are causing frustration, breeding negativity and killing creativity. Your challenge here is to remove the sources of stress if possible, and if not possible, to modify them in some way as to minimize their negative impact.

The "O" stands for the strategies that are used to take care of **Ourselves**. These are more than just offering the occasional yoga or massage class. These strategies are the health practices and information that can buffer your team members and positively impact their health. Often it is not possible for you to remove or modify a source of stress within your team, such as a plant closing or a tight deadline—it is what it is. You need to develop your team to ensure that they have a wide variety of coping options open to them in order to minimize the impact. These could include nutrition, exercise and relaxation strategies. Many leaders implement stretch breaks, light breaks and vent-outs. The "O" represents those strategies that take care of your physical needs and those that can give you a physical and mental break away from the challenges that are faced. These strategies are critical as they provide and restore your team's energy.

The last "S" stands for building **Support**. You see the need people have to share and get connected through the informal gatherings and the pre-meeting chatter. An effective leader takes this and makes it strategic. They set up mentors, their door is open, they encourage team gatherings, they provide places to get information and they assure complete confidence in sensitive matters. These social resources allow people to share, learn and unload their stress. They help them to feel connected and not isolated. They assist them to problem solve, keep their creativity and stay engaged. It is a major buffer against the challenges and sources of stress that are faced in the workplace.

When you keep this holistic SOS approach in mind, you effectively address the sources of stress that your team is facing, help to buffer them against the impact of that stress and provide support and opportunities to learn and share from each other.

The Seven Spokes of Organizational Wellness

Organizations will always face bumps in the road, but by building a strong wheel, your organization will move surely along the road to success. There are seven main focus areas within your organization that this SOS approach can be applied to in order to develop an effective, comprehensive plan and not a piecemeal approach. Each of these areas functions as a spoke within our wagon wheel. Failure to address all of these spokes weakens the entire wheel and the overall health of your organization.

You have seen it happen: You try to increase communication around an upcoming change in response to comments that no one lets anyone know what is going on—only to have the negativity increase. Later, you find out that the real issue is the lack of updated technology to get the job done right; the new planned change does nothing to address their frustrations.

All seven spokes of your business must be examined and addressed to be effective. What is *causing* stress in these areas? What strategies are your team using to deal with these stressors? What strategies would *buffer* them against these stressors? What *supports* do they need? When you look at the issues within each of your business spokes that can cause stress, you will begin to formulate a plan on how to have a positive and lasting impact on the health of your team and organization.

1. **L**iving healthy
2. **E**nvironment
3. **A**ttaining balance
4. **D**ynamics and culture
5. **E**mployee services
6. **R**emuneration and benefits
7. **S**upport building

1. Living healthy: In an ideal world, stressful periods were to be followed by energy-restoring phases such as naps or sharing meals. Today that is not realistic. What we find is that employees and leaders get so caught up in the situations that are stressful that they often forget about the simple techniques that can be done to restore their body's natural rhythm and decrease the negative effects that stress can have on them. The unhealthy lifestyles that some members of your team may be choosing or experiencing may also be the source of their stress.

Using the SOS approach, can you identify situations that may be adding stress to your team? And if yes, can you remove or modify these in any way? Are over-time or shift cycles causing your team to be sleep deprived? Is there a lack of food or drink choices on-site that may be leading to unhealthy choices?

Simple areas in which you can assist your team in developing the "O" of SOS include the promotion of proper sleeping, eating and exercising habits. You can offer your team this valuable health information in a number of ways, including workshops, handouts, posters, quick e-mails, and e-news briefs. You can support these activities by ensuring access to water coolers, juice dispensers, vending machines with low-calorie snack choices, and by having your cafeteria highlight healthy food choices.

Support, the last "S," may mean encouraging a buddy system to minimize the impact of sleepiness, especially in your 24-hour operations. Even though most of

Awakening the Workplace

your teams know that they can take a break or go for a walk if they need to, vocalizing this regularly and encouraging those employees who seem tired or frustrated can go along way to restoring their energy.

You also must be able to utilize the top four strategies for living healthy—breathing, "deskercises," energy strategies and humor—to restore your own energy. The great thing about these four basics is that they are fast and easy to use:

Breathe In, Breathe Out

Air is the primary "food" of our body. Rapid, shallow breathing is a common involuntary reaction to stress and causes you to feel tired and foggy-headed. Deep breathing interrupts this response and can be a powerful means of recharging yourself and regaining a more natural rhythm. Sit back—breathe slowly, filling the bottom portion of your lungs—then the middle—finally the top—hold—then slowly release the top—then the middle—and finally the bottom. Do 5 to 10 of these regularly throughout the day to revive your energy. You can also use this method to relieve your headaches, relax your shoulders, quiet your racing thoughts, and turn restlessness into calmness. You can purposefully utilize this strategy to engage your team prior to problem solving or to refocus them during chaos. Take a few moments and encourage them to breathe.

One More, Two More

Tense muscles cause blood to be squeezed out of the body tissue, resulting in oxygen and nutrient depletion and causing pain and a lack of concentration. "Deskercises" or self-massage can be helpful in releasing tension and restoring the flow of blood. Try some of these quick examples during your breaks or after meetings. Slowly roll your neck from side to side in a neck roll. Squeeze your shoulders up towards your ears for a shoulder shrug. Stand up and slowly swing your hips in a clockwise then counter-clockwise motion called hip twisters. Don't forget your wrists if you do a lot of keyboarding, or quarter squats if you spend a lot of time sitting or standing in one place. These "deskercises" can relax your muscles, increase your focus for problem solving and revitalize your energy. This is a great strategy to recapture some energy in the middle of a difficult team meeting.

Garbage In, Garbage Out

During challenging times it is not uncommon for you or your team to compromise or completely forget about eating, rehydrating and getting outside for some fresh air and light. These activities are an integral part of our energy system and a caring leader knows how to utilize their benefits. Ensure that your meetings have enough breaks built into them, provide nutritious rather that high-sugar snacks, and opt for waters and juices instead of coffee and sodas, even though initially they may not be the first choice of your participants. Examine their workspaces to see if they are adequately lit and encourage your employees to get outdoors for fresh air and an infusion of natural light.

Smile and the World Will Join You

Your mood and behavior drives the moods and behaviors of your team. Moods are contagious and laughter is the most contagious of them all. Start with making sure you are in an optimistic and high-energy mood. Humor and optimism create a climate where information sharing, trust, healthy risk taking and learning flourish. Build a sense of fun into the day and you will be rewarded with increased productivity and highly engaged members.

Focusing on these top four living healthy tips, and this spoke in general, will ensure that you and your employees have the energy and self-management strategies to deal with the challenges along your way.

2. Environment: Historically, the main focus of this spoke was minimizing stressful environmental situations, such as workplace hazards. You have probably been involved in a first-aid, CPR or WHMIS course. You must go beyond these basic environmental situations and examine such issues as the availability of the appropriate resources in order for your team to do their jobs. Do they need updated software or communication tools? Do they need further training on this new technology? Examine workstation ergonomics, air quality and signage to see if they are causing additional levels of frustration or a negative impact on the health of your team. Help them to buffer themselves as these changes are made, for example, by setting up a specific ergonomics exercise program or providing an outlet to express their concerns.

3. Attaining balance: Work-life balance strategies help the employee to manage the hectic pace and various responsibilities of their life. Do your company demographics and your team's personal stories give you clues as to the balance situations that they are finding stressful? Provide them with childcare and eldercare information from your local community organizations if you are dealing with parents or with employees who are in the sandwich generation. Show understanding for their appointments and family illness challenges through personal responsibility leave or flex-time, or allow telecommuting and job sharing, if realistic. Understand that balance is a prime motivator to your employees. You may need to support them by becoming the company advocate for childcare and eldercare workshops, alternative work arrangements, or the hiring of an Employee Assistance Provider (EAP) to allow your team an alternate opportunity to confidentially discuss their issues.

4. Dynamics and culture: Jim's story is a classic example of where the workplace culture and the dynamics created by the new boss had an enormous negative impact. Jim faced unclear job expectations, criticism, lack of input into decision making, work overload, lack of connection to the corporate goals, and a lack of recognition and appreciation.

Caring leaders create trust, commitment and positive communication through a continued examination of workplace dynamics and culture. Is there stress over your hiring practices? Do they result in the wrong person being hired or are they based on favoritism? Supportive leaders focus on hiring practises that ensure that the right person is hired for the right job. Are deadlines unrealistic, making your team feel that they are always behind? Help team members to set priorities and advocate for more realistic deadlines. Help them to buffer and restore their energy against these deadlines, conflicts, complicated policies and procedures by ensuring that they take their vacation allotment. Our studies show that a majority of employees return from their vacations re-energized and feeling better about their jobs. Can you support them by providing incentives and rewards for good work? Rewards may range from a public thank you to time off. Be creative. If money is tight, check out the Internet, where you will find lots of low-cost or no-cost rewards. Encourage feedback. This will let them know that you are there for them and that support is available.

5. Employee services: Access to various on-site health services can detect and head off health issues before they become serious. An employee health assessment may indicate the need for on-site blood pressure, cholesterol, glucose, prostate or breast screening programs. You may need to advocate for immunization and flu shots or access to information or presentations on diabetes, stomach disorders, arthritis and pain control. This is where listening to your team will give you clues as to the health challenges they are facing. You may need to encourage the use of these resources, as there is a certain amount of stigma associated with many of these illnesses. Your support may give someone the strength to get the information that they need and to minimize its impact.

6. Remuneration and health benefits: Of the top attractors for employees, we know that competitive base pay and an adequate healthcare benefits package are always included. Showing respect for your team means ensuring that your employees are fairly compensated for their efforts both within your company and in the broader scope of your industry. Often, there is a lack of awareness about what is included under the subsidies and alternative healthcare coverage. Bring in a benefits representative to answer questions and provide specific examples.

7. Support building: A great deal of your life and your team's life is spent at work, and your workplace can either promote or discourage the valuable opportunity to share and learn from each other. This support building spoke blends into many of the strategies of your other spokes. But, just as the Support in our SOS approach to organizational and employee wellness is one of the three keys, support building requires special attention. Are you building a team of committed and engaged employees? Team-building strategies can range from the practical to the fun. Check in with your team to see how they are doing. Encourage face-to-face communication. Praise their successes. Celebrate important occasions and milestones. Incorporate community activities. Issue fun challenges. Get them laughing together.

Weathering the Bumps

Though many of these individual areas within our Seven Spokes of Organizational Wellness have been explored, researched and widely publicized, they are often not pulled back together to give today's leader a clear picture of what areas need to be addressed to promote a positive workplace culture and to strengthen organizational wellness. By addressing all seven spokes, you will build a team that can navigate the bumpy road ahead.

Address the "S" of the SOS approach to organizational and employee wellness. Use the Seven Spokes to discover the situations and sources of stress your team members are facing. Next, help them to buffer themselves against the impact of that stress and provide them with support.

» Jim moved on to a new company and became the new boss. He wanted to be successful, so he took the time to learn about each member of his team and to discover what they liked and didn't like about their jobs. He utilized this information and developed a plan.

Jim knew that he had the biggest role to play when addressing the workplace culture and the dynamics of the team. He updated his team on the projects they were working on and gave a clear picture of the larger corporate goals. He asked them for suggestions on how to improve the way work was accomplished and asked for feedback on new initiatives that were being considered by the company. Great suggestions came forward and he found out that what they really needed were some of their machines replaced. He included this in the upcoming budget, along with the resources for training on these machines. He also found that there were some ergonomic concerns around their workstations. He had the necessary adjustments made.

He discovered that meetings had become more of an annoyance and were seen as time-wasters. Jim implemented meetings that were more goal focused and action oriented. These action points were placed onto an on-line master plan so that they could be continually updated. This eventually allowed the team to feel connected. E-mail and the urgency that was connected to it were also leading to frustration and resentment. Together, they came up with a code that was attached to each message that represented its urgency. They also laid out ground rules for copying each other on messages, where and how these documents were filed and updated, and how frequently e-mail was to be checked

Jim realized that they had never celebrated anything, so he surprised team members with a luncheon and company T-shirts for their next successful product launch. Even though it wasn't elaborate, he heard several comments appreciating the break and the time to just get together. He followed this up with a series of fun and simple challenges where they could win points to be exchanged for prizes. He was amazed at how simple yet effective these challenges were at overcoming the afternoon slump and engaging the team for the rest of the day.

Jim's team was evenly split between young parents and experienced grandparents. Each group had very different balance issues. He worked with HR to bring in a speaker to present ideas and strategies for parenting and another on effectively dealing with intergenerational conflict. Both lunch 'n' learns went well.

Jim had a knack for losing himself in his work and not taking his own breaks. He knew that his actions spoke volumes. This was the hardest area for him to address, but if he was going to encourage healthy behaviors, he needed to be the first one to model them. He started with a few stretch breaks and invited others to join him for a quick walk outside, as this always seemed to perk him up. He wanted to eat healthier and cut back on caffeine, so he brought in a juice dispenser, moved the coffee machine out of the high-traffic area, got rid of the pop machine entirely, and had the vending company replace the cookies and chips with healthier snacks. He pushed himself beyond his comfort zone and implemented deep-breathing strategies. It felt awkward at first, but eventually it became second nature.

Jim and his team were successful. They were energized, and one employee confided that she wasn't as tired and drained when she went home to her family. In just a couple of months, absenteeism dropped and they were producing outstanding results. **«**

Jim was creating a workplace that was based on respect and employees that were engaged. He was beginning to address the Situations—those things that were frustrating his team. He personally started to take better care of himself by eating right, taking breaks and getting more sleep, and he could see how his team was also focusing more on the "O" (Ourselves). They were no longer a group of individuals; he was building an environment of team Support. SOS in action!

Leadership is important in assuring and developing organizational health.

Healthy, engaged employees positively benefit the bottom line, and leaders are in the best position to create a set of practices that promote employee engagement, health and organizational success. The SOS approach to organizational and employee wellness works. Successful, caring leaders discover the sources of stress, help to buffer their team against the impact of that stress and provide them with support.

Today's successful companies purposefully build leaders and teams to weather the many bumps in the road. Awareness of organizational health is key. When everyone in the organization is focused on creating a healthy work environment and promoting healthy lifestyles, the organization will be productive, effective and competitive. The SOS approach applied to the Seven Spokes of Organizational Wellness will carry your company safely along the bumpy road, while your competitors are left wondering how to fix their flat tire.

Beverly Beuermann-King

Beverly Beuermann-King is a stress and wellness specialist who translates current research and best practices information into a realistic, accessible and practical approach to assist leaders and their teams in dealing with today's complex and stressful issues. Her expertise has led her to become an in-demand speaker for more than 25,000 business leaders and teams during the past 15 years, and a sought-after media personality through more than 60 interviews each year. She is the only stress and wellness specialist to also have been an education consultant to the Canadian Mental Health Association.

Beverly's most sought-after presentations include Spring Into Action—Harness Your Energy; Stress Basics—Lessons From the Cave Dweller; Handling Negative Attitudes and Difficult People Without Becoming Stressed Out; and Stress Smarts for Leaders—Assessing Team Member Stress. Her programs are consistently rated excellent for relevance, content and high-energy presentation style.

Beverly has written many articles and is the author of the widely distributed employee wellness best practices e-newsletter *Path to Wellness*. Her personal experience in partnering, parenting and care giving, along with running her own company, helps her to bring a realistic view to employing practical solutions in order to Work Smart and Live Smart.

Business Name:	Work Smart Live Smart, R 'n' B Consulting
Address:	211 Fingerboard Road, Little Britain, ON K0M 2C0
Telephone:	705-786-0437
E-mail:	info@WorkSmartLiveSmart.com
Web Address:	www.WorkSmartLiveSmart.com
Professional Affiliations:	Canadian Association of Professional Speakers—Toronto Chapter board member; National Speakers Association; International Federation of Professional Speakers

Laura Min Jackson, MSOD

Nia Harmony

Head, Heart and Wallet:
A Model for Compassionate Listening
in the Workplace

Consider your last important decision. Did you make it primarily because it made the most sense intellectually? Was it an emotional response to a situation, or was it based on a gut feeling? Perhaps you made your decision primarily because of a financial motivation behind the issue.

By looking at what's behind our thinking, we take a step toward better understanding how we process information, make decisions and take action. Gaining insight into whether we allow ourselves to be influenced primarily by our intellect, emotions or financial considerations is the key. If we are ruled by our intellect and driven by rational thought and logic, it is called the Head driver. If the Heart driver is active, it symbolizes the emotional realm and includes decisions and actions that are based on beliefs, values and feelings. Then there is the Wallet driver, which encompasses not just the financial perspective, but also our personal sense of abundance or scarcity, and our perceptions of possible cost, loss or gain.

Characteristics of the Head, Heart and Wallet Drivers

Driver	Characteristics
Head	Based on rational thought and logic
Heart	Based on beliefs, values and feelings
Wallet	Based on perceptions of possible cost, loss or gain, abundance or scarcity

These drivers seldom operate in isolation—we're rarely 100 percent emotional or 100 percent rational in our decision-making—and it's important to note that there are no "right" or "wrong" drivers. We may flexibly employ them in response to different situations. They work in combination with one another, with one dominant at any one time. While evaluating every decision against all three drivers wouldn't be productive, it is useful to know our tendencies to favor one for most circumstances, and to consider how well that's serving us. For example, if I'm aware of a preference to consistently, rationally consider a number of factors before I make a decision, then I can choose to test my flexibility by also occasionally checking my feelings at an emotional level, taking a quick "gut check" to affirm my intellectual position.

Head, Heart and Wallet at Work

The Head

An individual who works primarily from the realm of the Head will make decisions and choices based primarily on the intellectual realm. When we are thoughtful, deliberative, and rely on data and analysis to make decisions, our Head is leading. In the workplace, many decisions are driven from rational models. Working from the Head enables us to efficiently sort and prioritize different kinds of information, and this approach is often the safest choice. Working from the Head can be efficient, as it encourages systematic, logical approaches. The Head also encompasses mental creativity, thereby contributing important dimensions of brainstorming, theorizing and troubleshooting.

From an organizational perspective, most North American firms operating today place a priority on achieving key goals and specific performance metrics, measuring output, productivity, efficiency, and the like. Companies that emphasize operational excellence are likely to reward and reinforce employees and managers who conduct themselves primarily from the perspective of the Head, that is, those who deliver work product and make decisions primarily from the rational, logical and intellectual realm.

The Heart

This driver symbolizes the emotional realm, and includes decisions and actions an individual takes while operating primarily from their beliefs, values or feelings. When we are choosing based on our intuition, personal principles or "gut" feeling, our Heart is the primary driver. In some workplaces, the expression of emotions or reliance on intuition can be discouraged, but abandoning the realm of the Heart altogether can create a working environment that is cold, stifling and mechanistic.

Bringing the Heart into the workplace can enhance its sense of humanity; employees who work in an environment that incorporates the Heart driver may have higher satisfaction, engagement and commitment to the organization's overall mission. Moreover, leaders who work effectively with their Heart dimension can more easily appeal to the Heart perspective in others, enabling them to more effectively inspire and motivate, and generate deep passion, commitment and loyalty. This can be particularly important for service-sector organizations, where the work output focuses on fulfilling the needs of customers outside of the organization, and success is often linked to repeat business from loyal customers. Many customer loyalty studies indicate it's the experience of consistently receiving "that something extra" that differentiates companies from the rest of the field, and I believe it's when an organization successfully connects to a customer's Heart driver that this distinctive experience is created and reinforced.

The Wallet

In today's economically challenged environment, when it seems everyone is being asked to do more with fewer resources, and the standards for financial performance are being continually elevated, many firms are increasingly emphasizing the Wallet driver. Realizing greater cost efficiencies, making investment decisions based on calculated returns, and consistently achieving aggressive financial goals, quarter after quarter, are requisite in today's investor-centric business environment, and operating from the Wallet generally encourages rapid decision making and increased efficiencies. Yet, while economics play a vital role in today's business decision making, it is counterbalanced by the risk of achieving short-term gains without adequate consideration for longer term organizational and strategic consequences.

Importantly, the Wallet dimension encompasses not only the financial perspective and perceptions of possible cost, loss or gain, but also our personal sense of abundance or scarcity. Consider the choices we make if we believe our time, resources or options are inadequate and that we must preserve what little we have. We begin operating from a scarcity perspective; and operating with a great need to hold tightly to what we have or risk losing it, can powerfully influence our behaviors and decisions. Conversely, working from a position of abundance, of believing we have enough, and that, individually, we *are* enough, can open up a world of possibilities.

Making Decisions: My Head, Heart and Wallet Drivers

The following three-part assessment is an opportunity to engage in self-reflection and explore the three drivers' presence in your life. It is recommended that you complete this assessment a couple of times—now and another time later—to see whether your responses vary at all. This is because most people tend to stay in their Head realm while reading, an appropriate mode for absorbing and incorporating new information. Being in the Head mode, however, may overly influence your responses at this time, which is why reconsidering these questions again at a future time, preferably after you have engaged in another kind of activity, may provide additional insight.

Circle the response that you believe is most true for you, most of the time.

1. **When it comes to decision making, I tend to...**
   a. Rely on facts and data to aid my decision making
   b. Decide based on what feels right
   c. Choose based on what will yield the best outcome for me personally
   d. Other:

2. **When responding to a crisis, I'm best at...**
   a. Diagnosing what happened
   b. Making sure the people involved are taken care of
   c. Encouraging quick resolution
   d. Other:

3. **On my work performance assessment, I would be most proud if my boss recognized my...**
   a. Problem-solving skills
   b. Ability to motivate others
   c. Sound financial performance
   d. Other:

4. **If I were assessing the possibility of enacting a reduction-in-force or layoff at my workplace, my first question would be...**
   a. What would be involved?
   b. Who would be impacted?
   c. How much it would cost?
   d. Other:

5. **In my current workplace, I'm most likely to be rewarded for...**
   a. Problem solving and innovative thinking
   b. Organizational loyalty and commitment
   c. Achieving key financial goals
   d. Other:

If your responses to the above questions were primarily "a's," that indicates a tendency to rely most heavily on the Head; primarily "b's" corresponds to the Heart driver, and primarily "c's" are related to the Wallet driver. Please take the time to reflect on any responses where you wrote "d" and see how they relate, if at all, to the three primary drivers, or if you have identified yet another driver influencing your decision making. [Feedback on other drivers you may have identified for yourself is welcome and an e-mail address is available following this chapter.] After identifying your primary driver, you may also explore how your drivers manifest in your life by completing the following statements:

- I'm most likely to use my Head driver during the following circumstances:

- I'm most likely to use my Heart driver during the following circumstances:

- I'm most likely to use my Wallet driver during the following circumstances:

- The driver that is most valued by my workplace is:

- The driver that is least valued by my workplace is:

- Among the Head, Heart and Wallet, the driver that is most unfamiliar to me is _____ because:

Finally, to complete the assessment, answer the following questions that reflect on your completed statements above:

- Is there any disparity between your primary driver and what your organization appears to value?

- How does that feel to you?

- How might your organization's reward and recognition system influence how you invoke your primary driver, make decisions and take actions in the workplace?

- When considering both your primary driver and the one you noted as least familiar to you, what are the implications for how you make decisions?

- When might you be better served by using a less familiar driver?

Exploring Deeper Interpersonal Connections

Equipped now with some additional understanding of our personal preferences among the three drivers, we can now explore how the Head, Heart and Wallet model is present in our interpersonal relationships at work.

Think back to a recent time when you truly felt listened to at work. Perhaps it was a few minutes shared with a colleague to celebrate the successful completion of an important assignment, or a conversation with a key stakeholder in which you were able to successfully reach consensus regarding a challenging project. It's likely you felt understood and appreciated by those with whom you were interacting. You may have felt a sense of connection, mutual respect and regard for one another.

Now recall a situation when you felt frustrated, disconnected or out-of-sync with your colleagues. Perhaps you and another associate had different ideas about how to address an important problem, or you didn't share similar views on a key strategic issue. If the situation continued unresolved and tensions rose, there's a chance that both parties became more entrenched and the divergent opinions blossomed into a more defined conflict. You both may have felt angry, anxious and misunderstood; in the escalating mutual frustration, one of you might actually have said, "You're not listening to what I'm saying!"

Compassionate Listening

At work, and in other areas of our life, everyone wants to feel heard—we all want acknowledgment when we express ourselves. This is true when people are expressing opinions, when they are mentioning financial possibilities, and particularly when they are giving voice to their feelings. We can use the Head, Heart and Wallet model to become more active, compassionate listeners, giving us another means of enhancing our interpersonal relationships at work. If we can gain an understanding of another individual's orientation, then we have the option of responding from the same driver, if we so choose. Compassionate listening with others can be practiced at any time; the primary requirement is that we temporarily suspend our own hopes, fears and agendas, and dedicate our energy to more completely receiving the message being sent by the other party. We substitute curiosity, non-judgmental observation and personal openness for the filtering, comparing, dreaming or advising that we might customarily indulge in—practices that prohibit our active listening and result in maintaining interpersonal connections at more superficial levels. Central to the practice of compassionate listening is committing ourselves to respecting the other individual and what they are contributing to the conversation.

To listen compassionately, we first make a commitment to actively listen, and we then focus our attention on receiving the speaker's message. We also listen for indications of their primary driver.

Are they conveying factual, straightforward information, or explaining their rationale for a particular decision or action? Chances are they are operating from the Head realm. Are they highly animated and expressing their feelings? It would appear the Heart is a considerable influencer. Are they mentioning concerns over cost, or focusing on calculated gains? These would indicate the Wallet as the primary driver. In compassionate listening, we are not performing psychoanalysis, nor are we judging whether their driver is "right" or "wrong." We accept the incoming information as data, not as evidence to support an assumption we may have been making. Our goal is to hear the other party and to listen for indications of their primary driver, because this enables us to acknowledge and choose whether to align our response in return. By choosing to listen compassionately, we risk making ourselves more vulnerable through our openness, and we are willing to take this risk for the possibility of greater understanding and connection with the other individual. We then choose our response, ensuring that we maintain personal authenticity and integrity in the exchange.

Conversations are most powerful when the parties' drivers are aligned; a speaker is more likely to feel connected, listened to and appreciated if you can authentically respond from a similar driver.

If someone is excitedly relating the tale of their latest workplace victory (Heart), and our response is grounded in our preferred driver of rationality (Head), we miss an opportunity for connection. Over time, if it happens consistently, this kind of mismatch can erode the depth and quality of a working relationship. At the same time, we must maintain personal authenticity while listening compassionately. It is entirely possible to acknowledge the other speaker's driver, and maintain personal integrity in our response, and it's critical to do so. Our objective is to align the drivers, Head to Head, Heart to Heart, and Wallet to Wallet, in our response, but not to merely parrot back what we believe the other party wants to hear. People want to feel listened to; if we provide an artificially manufactured response in an attempt to match their enthusiasm, while deep down we have grave misgivings, it can be more damaging to the relationship and to our personal integrity than if we had expressed our genuine thoughts and feelings.

Finally, one fundamental of compassionate listening is noticing whether there are any disconnects between the speaker's expression of feelings or emotions and their physical presentation. This can be especially common in the workplace, where logic and rationality are highly valued, and people are more likely to have been socialized to mask their emotions. As a compassionate listener, we can experience this disconnect as a misalignment between "the words and the music"—for example, someone discussing a topic that aggravates them, in which they might verbalize emotions ("That really ticked me off") but speak in a complete monotone. Conversely, they may say, "Everything's fine," but you notice some indications in their non-verbal communications that they are experiencing stress.

If you encounter misalignment situations and are listening compassionately, you can ask a question or make a non-judgmental observation, such as, "That sounds very stressful," which provides an invitation for more disclosure from the other speaker. If they choose not to respond, it's probably an indication that they are uncomfortable disclosing further, and in the spirit of compassion, you realize that further probing would not alleviate their discomfort, so it's best to let it go. What's key is that you remained present, listening, available and open throughout the exchange.

A Checklist for Compassionate Listening

- First, commit yourself to listening to what is being said. Provide appropriate cues to indicate you are listening, for example, nodding, paraphrasing, asking appropriate questions to further the dialogue.

- Listen closely for cues indicating the other speaker's primary driver. Are they speaking from a logical, rational realm? From an emotional realm? From a sense of scarcity or abundance?

- Determine whether you can respond from the corresponding driver—Head, Heart or Wallet.

- Practice compassion with yourself; if you find yourself assuming, diagnosing, judging or engaging in other unproductive listening practices, notice and release them without self-criticism, and immediately return your attention to the speaker.

My Compassionate Listening Abilities

What follows is a brief self-assessment that can be used to evaluate your success in practicing compassionate listening. If you wish to track your progress, you may revisit this assessment over time, to determine changes in your experience as you continue working on listening compassionately. If appropriate, you may also seek feedback from the other party. You might consider asking how the other person is feeling after your exchange, when they felt most listened to by you, or if they have suggestions on what you can do next time to further improve your listening skills.

Reflecting Upon Compassionate Listening

1. After practicing compassionate listening, I realized…
2. I felt most connected during the conversation when…
3. I did well when…
4. I was able to maintain my personal authenticity when…
5. I want to further develop my ability to…
6. The listening blocks that I tend to use most are…
7. I find it easiest to practice compassionate listening with…
8. I find it most challenging to practice compassionate listening with…
9. The feedback I received from the other party was…

Tools During Conflict

The practice of compassionate listening can be at its most powerful during conversations that are highly charged with emotion, conflict or controversy. These are the likely situations when we might ordinarily seek to defend ourselves, thereby curtailing our involvement in the dialogue and our openness to hearing the messages being conveyed.

> **Much of the interpersonal conflict we experience**
> **at work, as well as in other areas of our life, can**
> **escalate when the parties' drivers as misaligned.**

Understanding our personal preferred driver (Head, Heart or Wallet) and practicing compassionate listening should help us move closer toward achieving mutual understanding, which is key to resolving virtually all conflicts. Compassionate listening can help us more constructively resolve conflicts because it encourages us to direct energy toward similar goals, rather than work in opposition. Importantly, this does not mean abandoning our position and capitulating to the other person's point of view; whether or not we actually agree with their position becomes secondary to a higher goal of achieving greater understanding and connectedness while working toward resolution. Central to this approach is our willingness to release personal attachment to "winning" the conflict, and to reframe the situation as one where resolving the situation is our ultimate goal.

In conflict situations, we can begin by using the Head, Heart and Wallet model to perform a quick personal check-in:

- Where am I on this issue? What's driving my conviction of my position?
- Is my Head driving this situation? Do I believe the other person has their facts wrong or is misinterpreting the information?
- Is my Heart leading the way? What feelings do I have about this person and this situation?
- Is there an element of Wallet driving this? How great is the loss if I don't prevail in this conflict?

There are three important considerations about interacting during conflict. Firstly, when exploring these questions, it will serve you best if you can work from the realm of Head, which can be particularly challenging, since conflict situations almost always invoke some emotions, which could catalyze our Heart driver. Secondly, conflicts may be one of the few situations where emotions are considered acceptable in the workplace, and they, therefore, may carry a disproportionately greater significance as one of the few available organizational "release valves."

A third consideration is a common tendency to underestimate the power of our Wallet driver in conflict situations. We may believe that our disagreement is based entirely on principle, and while principles are an important component in conflict, another key element relates to our personal fears. As conflict escalates, we often become entrenched in our positions due to some sense of scarcity. We may fear losing a conflict because it can negatively impact our workplace status. We may be averse to suffering a loss in a competitive sense, or we might fear that losing the conflict could translate to a greater rejection of ourselves in the workplace. Regardless of what fear or potential loss the conflict situation is triggering in us, it is well worth taking the time to explore and acknowledge it.

Once we are clear on our personal position, any fears we are experiencing, and the drivers influencing us, we may use the questions associated with our check-in as the basis for starting to understand the other party's position. As we listen to the other party, we can check to see if we understand what is driving the conviction of their position. We may then listen for any indication of their Head, Heart or Wallet driver. Remember that in conflict conversations, the drivers may change quickly and repeatedly, requiring greater active listening and flexibility. We must remain committed to resolving the conflict, and focused on listening and gaining data, so that we can understand the other party's position and their driver. This is a time for as much openness and flexibility as we can muster. Our opportunity to respond will be forthcoming, but while the other party is expressing their position, it's best to allow the space for them to do so as fully as possible. This is also an important time for us to be mindful of any listening blocks we may be employing—it's a natural tendency to listen selectively when we are in conflict situations, but it doesn't necessarily serve our higher goal of achieving constructive resolution.

During the conflict conversation, we should work to play back and paraphrase what we are hearing, so that the speaker feels heard or can make any necessary corrections. We can also ask questions to gain greater clarity on the speaker's primary driver. An example of this might be, "I hear you saying X, Y and Z about the project. I also hear you saying you're very disappointed about the results we've seen thus far. What else are you feeling about this situation?" This offers an invitation for the speaker to disclose further, thereby elaborating on their position and their driver. Conversely, when we are speaking, it helps to keep our comments framed in what is happening to us, and to explicitly reference the primary driver behind our position. Here are some examples:

- "After looking at the data, my conclusion is..." (Head)
- "In this situation, I feel..." (Heart)
- "My concerns about this relate to the financial consequences of..." (Wallet)

Finally, at the conclusion of any conflict discussion, it may be helpful for us to reflect back on the questions previously presented under "Reflecting Upon Compassionate Listening" (page 182), to evaluate what we did effectively, and those areas we may wish to focus on for future improvement. When were we able to best maintain personal authenticity, and when did we find it most challenging to do so? Can we identify the listening blocks we employed? What did we do well, and in what areas would we like to improve? And finally, when did we feel fear during the situation, and what was it related to?

The next time you hear the words, "You're not listening to me!" embrace it as an opportunity to engage the Head, Heart and Wallet model and practice compassionate listening. Whether in conflict or agreement, when interacting with others or evaluating situations on our own, we always have the option to explore our Head, Heart and Wallet drivers to better understand ourselves and to identify opportunities to further enhance our individual and interpersonal effectiveness.

Laura Min Jackson

Laura Min Jackson is an award-winning writer and consultant, specializing in organization leadership, change and communications. As a certified teacher of The Nia Technique® and founder of Nia Harmony, she is dedicated to helping individuals, groups and organizations achieve greater health, creativity and growth.

Laura has worked in both successful start-ups and international consultancies, and most recently, she helped launch a Fortune 1000/Midcap 400 company. As a professional speaker, Laura has presented to groups and organizations that include The Conference Board, Columbia University, Women in Thoracic Surgery, and Il Foro Cardiovascular. Her consulting expertise includes change management and leadership, branding and crisis/conflict communications. She also provides individualized coaching for enhancing personal and professional effectiveness.

Laura is also an adjunct faculty member at California State University (Fullerton), and is co-author of the upcoming book *Working With Heart: Your Guide to Choices in Work* and Life (www.workingwithheart.com). She holds a BA in Communications, and an MSOD from Pepperdine University. Laura is a member of IDEA, the Health Fitness Association and the Global Communications Forum.

Business Name:	Nia Harmony
Address:	2913 El Camino Real #806, Tustin, CA USA 92782
Telephone/fax:	714-731-6761
E-mail:	laura@niaharmony.com
Web site:	www.niaharmony.com
Professional affiliations:	California Faculty Association

Favorite Quote
There's treasure everywhere!
—Bill Watterson

Gina Lavery

Synchronicity Partners

Leadership Challenge:
Energy Crisis in the Workplace

Leaders struggle to be effective in a world that expects perfection, mastery and authenticity. Living with constant change, where cellphones, Blackberries and the Internet continually increase the intensity and quantity of demands from co-workers, bosses, employees, family members and friends, leaders barely have a chance to accomplish what they set out to do on a daily basis. While adopting new methods of dealing with these challenges may produce results, they may also occur as something *more* to do. Ironically, leaders may put off any development activities until they have the time, which may result in indefinite postponement.

In addition to managing their own development, leaders are responsible for maximizing employee effectiveness and productivity. To achieve ever more challenging goals, leaders require a workforce that is "awake," meaning they are engaged, energized, productive and contributing close to 100 percent of its potential. Yet, according to a Gallup poll, 70 percent of the US workforce is "asleep" or disengaged, meaning employees are not enthusiastic or motivated, are emotionally detached and wasting time. These disengaged workers are not working even close to their capacity.

Imagine if your car started only once out of every three times you turned the key in the ignition—that's the equivalent of what's happening in today's workforce.

While some leadership techniques or strategies may help to temporarily increase engagement and productivity, employees are likely to return to their original state of drowsiness, inattention and apathy all too soon. Clearly, there's an "energy crisis" in the workplace, and fortunately, leaders can do something about it. By cultivating new sources of energy, leaders can re-energize the workforce and stimulate employees to do the same for themselves.

Many leadership techniques employ extrinsic motivators, such as money, promotion or status—factors that may prevent short-term dissatisfaction, but do not tend to influence lasting fulfillment and satisfaction. By contrast, intrinsic rewards, which provide a sense of achievement, autonomy or self-knowledge, are more likely to tap into employees' own renewable energy sources—their sense of satisfaction, fulfillment, aspiration and purpose—and thus keep them engaged, inspired and awake. If the key to achieving superior and lasting business results is engaged employees, then leaders must find a way to consistently access employees' intrinsic energy sources. Leaders can start the process by identifying, cultivating and redirecting their own energy sources, which will then create optimal conditions for employees to do the same. Leading in this way reframes the role of leadership to be harnessing organizational energy for maximum effectiveness.

Become an Energy Detective

Energy in the workplace can be found in five areas: physical, intellectual, emotional, spiritual and relational. As you review the table that follows, you may become aware of areas that are providing optimal energy, areas that may represent an untapped resource, or areas that drain energy. Also consider that a difficult situation *outside* work, such as a divorce or death, will most likely drain a person's energy *inside* work, debunking the myth that we can separate our work and personal lives. In reality, energy easily flows between work and personal life, and optimal energy is achieved from satisfaction and fulfillment in both domains. In spite of this principle, this chapter will focus primarily on workplace challenges.

Energy Sources, Drains and Blocks in the Workplace

Areas	Potential source	Potential drain	Pay attention to
Physical Related to health, appearance or physical environment	• Clean and uncluttered office • Adequate light and ventilation • Good health • Adequate sleep and exercise	• Messy office • Behind on annual health checkups • Working long hours • Lack of physical exercise	Flow, aesthetics and organization
Intellectual Thoughts, projects and ideas	• Stimulating conversation • Advanced education • Learning new skills • Open communication • Motivating thoughts • Career goals	• Self-doubt • Anxiety about security or career • Criticism • Being overwhelmed • Distractions	Level of challenge or stimulation
Emotional Emotions and level of expression	• Positive emotions: joy, appreciation • Promotions • A job you love	• Negative emotions: anger, jealousy, resentment • Suppressed or withheld emotions • Demotions, involuntary lateral moves	Amount and frequency of expression
Spiritual Life purpose, well-being, satisfaction and fulfillment	• Meaningful career path • Aspiration • Gratitude • Meditation, reflection	• No career path • Inability to express gratitude • Unclear life purpose/direction	Fulfillment and satisfaction
Relational Connections to people, things or situations	• Effective relationships with boss, peers, co-workers • Participation in decision making	• Ineffective relationships • Changes in organization structure • Irritating co-workers	Quality and effectiveness of connections

As leaders, our challenge is to ensure that the energy we generate is positive and affirming, instead of negative and demotivating. Negative energy tends to create a downward spiral, driving up defensiveness and communication blocks, and adversely impacting creativity and productivity. Positive energy tends to have a rejuvenating quality, inspiring and motivating employees. Consider the impact when you receive a "flaming" e-mail or when you receive positive feedback about your participation in a project. Leaders must develop practices to ensure energy remains positive.

Unblocking Energy Exercise

The following exercise will help you become aware of the five energy areas that relate to your work and help you assess where energy blocks are and how they drain energy. You'll also ascertain which blocks are the most amenable to immediate change and which need longer-term strategies. This exercise can be used to define energy sources, drains and blocks in individuals, teams or entire organizations. Do this for yourself first, and then consider using it as a team exercise.

- Of the five energy areas (physical, intellectual, emotional, spiritual and relational, as listed in the previous chart), which two provide you with the greatest source of energy?
- Within your two chosen energy areas, name five examples of energy sources. Write down whatever comes to mind and be as specific as possible. If you get stuck, refer to the table for ideas.
- Of the five energy types, choose two that drain your energy.
- Within your two chosen energy types, name five examples of energy drains. Again, write down the first thing that comes to mind and use the table if you need ideas.
- What two energy drains could you eliminate from your work today? Tomorrow? Next week? Make a plan to remove these drains as soon as possible.
- What energy sources are you not fully tapping into? Refer to the table and get creative.
- Are there any energy types that are blocked? If so, what can you do to open them as a potential source of energy? You may want to plot your five energy examples for both sources and drains on a chart as a visual guide.
- What additional thoughts do you have about removing energy drains and blocks to lessen their impact on your work life?

Breathing Life Into Your Passion

A leader must be passionate about their own work before attempting to revive a team of disengaged employees. The instructional video shown on most commercial airliners offers a great illustration of this principle: in the event of an emergency, adults are instructed to put on their own oxygen masks, then their child's. As a leader, connecting to the source of your own passion will provide you with the leadership energy that you need to motivate and inspire others.

Doing this work of discovering and cultivating energy at work through your passion is one of your greatest responsibilities as a leader. Many leaders ignore or are unaware of this important role, failing to realize that being awake themselves provides an atmosphere wherein employees can discover and cultivate their own passion. This type of atmosphere causes a shift from employees complaining about their jobs to finding out what excites them. While leaders are responsible for providing the right climate, employees are ultimately responsible for taking action to make their jobs satisfying and fulfilling. The two working in tandem create a generative cycle in which greater levels of both professional achievement and personal fulfillment are possible.

Leadership Energy Exercise

This exercise will help you begin to find a powerful source of leadership energy, fueled by your own aspiration and passion. It is likely you discovered a source of energy from the first reflection exercise that you can build on now.

- What motivated you to be in your present line of work?
- Why did you choose this particular company? Department? Job?
- What do you love about your job?
- How does your current job satisfy your career aspirations?
- How does your current job allow you to express your passion or life purpose?

If your current job does not supply adequate passion or positive energy, or does not satisfy career aspirations, then you owe it to yourself and the people you lead, to find one that does. If you did not find answers to the reflection questions, allow them to work in the back of your mind as you go about your day. The answers will come to you.

> *Don't ask yourself what the world needs. Ask yourself what makes you come alive, and then go and do that. Because what the world needs is people who have come alive.*
>
> Harold Whitman

Do you know what your employees like to do? What are their aspirations, hopes, dreams and goals? Many managers cannot answer these simple questions about their employees. Getting interested in your employees is the first step toward cultivating their passion and career aspirations.

Begin by asking them what they love about their job. Be prepared to meet with one of these possible reactions: a) enthusiasm, b) shock or disbelief, c) polite cooperation, or d) a blank stare. These reactions may arise because the employee cannot believe someone cares enough to ask or is shocked because the words "love" and "job" are used in the same sentence. Perhaps the employee has never thought about their job in this way—or maybe he is truly enthusiastic about why he loves his job.

Over time, this simple question transforms the energy of an individual, a team and, eventually, an organization. Discussing ways in which employees can make their job more satisfying and fulfilling is an excellent way to get them engaged in their career goals. Focusing on the positives will not fix all of the problems, but it will foster an open environment and unleash an abundance of creativity to fix problems faster than you thought possible.

Leaders who focus on their employees' aspirations can expect happier and more satisfied employees, resulting in better work performance at an improved pace. As employees become self-motivated to make their jobs interesting and fulfilling, they assume responsibility to not only create their own career paths, but their own job satisfaction as well.

Cultivating Positive Energy From Aspirations

Step #1—Get interested in your employees: Ask them, "What do you love about your job?"

Step #2—Help employees discover their passion: Have them list the activities they currently perform on the job. Of these activities, which provide the most energy? Which activities drain their energy? Observe them working and take note of when they seem to be very energetic or when they "light up." Share your observations with them.

Step #3—Connect employees to each other: As they discover their passion and interests, cross-pollinate them so they can learn from each other. Passion is contagious.

Step #4—Find out what employees aspire to: Aspirations may change over time, but helping them cultivate and achieve aspirations in their present job, even if it means changing or expanding responsibilities, will ultimately unleash positive energy into the organization.

Step #5—Help them achieve aspirational goals: Ensure that an employee's current job allows them to live out at least part of their aspirations, and if not, encourage them to find one that will.

Step #6—Repeat the process: Be prepared to have this conversation more than once as aspirations are clarified through regular discussion and review.

Incorporating this practice into your routine or into regular reviews will result in engaged employees and a workplace that has an abundance of energy. Once employees embrace the process of cultivating personal aspirations in their jobs, they often are ready to pursue several different courses of action, such as:

- requesting additional job responsibilities that will stretch them and make their job more enjoyable;
- requesting participation on a special project;
- finding a new job;
- beginning an activity outside of work that will satisfy aspirations and become a source of energy *at work*.

The leadership energy cycle diagram that follows summarizes the positive momentum generated by employees when they cultivate aspirations at work. Aspirations generate a level of emotional expression, which in turn impacts engagement and becomes self-reinforcing. The result of this practice will be an increasing sense of fulfillment and engagement in one's work.

Leaders Energy Cycle

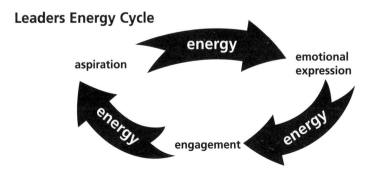

Be a Clearing House for Emotions

Emotions are energy, and naturally serve as an energy source or drain. Consider an employee who has lost a family member to cancer or one who has just returned from her honeymoon. These situations have the potential to deposit either negative or positive energy into the workplace. How does the smart leader harness the energetic potential these circumstances carry?

Emotions are vital to workplace engagement and productivity. Many of us have been taught that emotions and work do not mix, yet as humans, we are inherently emotional beings. We cannot simply leave our emotions at home. Emotions will always creep into the workplace, one way or another, and as leaders we need to channel their enormous energy potential. Fortunately, there is a growing body of research that proves the relationship between emotions and superior performance. Daniel Goleman, who popularized the concept of "emotional intelligence" found that managers who ignore emotions risk having unengaged, unhappy and unproductive employees. Goleman also discovered that CEOs create an emotional climate that directly impacts the moods of their direct reports and creates a ripple effect throughout the organization. He noted that leaders have a 50 percent impact on climate, which in turn has a 20 to 30 percent impact on business performance. Goleman's work clearly established a link between emotions and improved organizational performance.

Leaders who are committed to high performance, or who are planning major changes, need to acknowledge and harness emotional energy. Yet surfacing and allowing emotions in the workplace is rarely neat or orderly. Many leaders and employees have to unlearn the training that emotions and work don't mix and they must also access their own emotions, which can seem personally daunting. Training employees to express emotions instead of hiding them takes a courageous and confident leader.

Thank goodness for humor, one of the most effective and accepted workplace tools. Using humor effectively can shift emotions and relieve tension. Laughter engages people and tends to shift energy in a positive direction. One leader of a large healthcare firm routinely started off his "town hall" meetings with a funny story to put everyone at ease. His good humor engaged and attracted employees and his meetings were well-attended.

Listening is another way to help employees express emotions and redirect energy. Focused and intentional listening allows people to blow off steam, and the process of listening and venting can neutralize negative energy. Our natural tendency is to avoid angry employees, but as leaders we need to seek them out, listen to them and ask them to tell us more. As painful as this may seem, submerged anger is often counterproductive, dangerous and draining. Helping employees to transform this energy allows it to contribute to, rather than detract from, the workplace.

Emotional Energy Exercise

Familiarize yourself with your own untapped emotional energy by reflecting on the following questions. If you feel uncomfortable expressing or managing your own emotions, you may want to seek help through counseling, coaching, support groups or training.

- What is your current perspective on emotional expression in the workplace?
- What emotions are you more comfortable expressing in the workplace?
- What emotions are you less comfortable expressing?
- Are there any emotions that you suppress completely? Which ones?
- How can you create ways to infuse a sense of humor into the workplace?
- What steps can you take to strengthen your own level of emotional expression?
- How do you typically handle emotional expression by an employee?
- What can you do to create an environment that accepts emotional expression?

Relationships Are Everything

The main vehicle for creating and conveying energy at work is through relationships. Energy flows effortlessly across effective relationships, and gets blocked or stuck in relationships where difficulties have not been worked through. Through research I completed in 2004, I found that a key ingredient of personal fulfillment is the quality and nature of individual relationships. People become connected and related to each other while building and cultivating relationships, and thus become engaged. Negative relationships have the tendency to drain energy and create disengagement. People waste energy by engaging in gossip or by finding ways to avoid working with others. These types of activities drain enjoyment from the workplace. As leaders, we must take responsibility for transforming the energy dynamic in these negative relationships, and encourage others to do the same.

Relationship Reflection Exercise

- What do I believe to be true about relationships in the workplace?
- How do my relationships help or hinder my performance? Give an example of both an effective and ineffective relationship.
- In what ways might I manage relationships differently at work than I do outside of work? What relationship effectiveness skills outside work can I bring into the workplace?
- Is my energy at work more influenced by my effective relationships or ineffective relationships?
- With whom at work do I currently have issues? What actions can I take today to clear up these issues?

Appreciation and Gratitude

Busy executives often feel overwhelmed by the relationship aspects of leading. It is difficult to gauge how much time to spend in pursuit of positive workplace relationships. How can leaders efficiently cultivate positive energy in the shortest amount of time and get the biggest impact? Two ways that impact both the relational and emotional energy types and take very little time are appreciating your employees and being grateful for their unique talents and skills. Both appreciation and gratitude go beyond performance appraisals or formal recognition programs and yet can enhance the process of continuous workplace recognition.

When you take a moment during the course of a busy day to focus on what you appreciate about your employee, it provides a positive energy source for both of you. Routinely communicating your appreciation strengthens your relationship and also sends a clear message to them about their value. Being grateful is another way to shift energy. Reflecting on what you are most grateful for in the workplace taps into your spiritual energy source and allows positive energy to flow. These small, significant acts of expressing appreciation and gratitude will generate positive energy in your workplace. You may want to start by thinking about the unique talents and gifts your employee brings to his or her job, team and organization. You can also reflect on ways the employee has recently helped you with a work problem or issue. But, do not wait until their year-end review to share. Share your discoveries frequently and as they occur.

Provide Optimal Physical Conditions

Your physical work environment is either draining your energy or providing an energy wellspring. An organization where I once worked addressed the issue of rising operational costs by maximizing office utilization and crowding even more people into already tightly packed cubicles and offices. Not surprisingly, sales and profits lagged as the physical work environment drained energy and contributed to the negative impact on morale and productivity.

To create a healthy environment that generates positive energy, provide as much natural light as possible and make sure the building has a clean ventilation system, ideally with doors and windows that open to the outside. While many company officers pride themselves on large "corner" offices with lots of windows, there is a growing trend to give these offices to the staff employees. One organization in Chicago completely renovated its office so that windows were reserved for employee cubicles and conference rooms. The inside offices, away from the windows, were reserved for senior executives. All employees, even the inside executives, are now exposed to natural light, and benefit from this energy source.

Physical Environment Assessment Exercise

Take a moment now to scan your physical environment and answer the following reflection questions:
- As you take a "physical inventory," assess whether the environment provides adequate amounts of the following: natural light, ventilation, storage,

clean, uncluttered work surfaces, space to easily move between offices and cubicles.

- Notice whether or not employees are complaining about any problems or deficiencies in the physical environment. If so, what are they?
- What is one action you can take to improve the energy flow in your physical environment?

People need the right physical conditions to be engaged and productive. An optimal work space is an easy source of positive energy. Take actions now to ensure this vital resource is a source of energy for your employees.

Moving Your Energy Out of the Way

An often underutilized leadership strategy is to get out of the way. It requires learning what impedes progress and eliminating self-criticism, insecurities or old habits that have outlived their useful life and impair your leadership effectiveness. Working with a coach or therapist can help you discover your self-limiting paradigms and lessen their power and impact. If this is not an option, consider finding a trusted associate with whom you can talk freely and openly about these issues.

Once you begin to get out of your own way, you will find it easier to get out of others' way, which will open up positive energy flow. Instead of taking a hands-on approach, try a hands-off approach. Observe and listen; avoid telling your employees what to do. Once you understand what your employees need to produce results, you can spend your time removing obstacles instead of micromanaging.

» One new sales manager reported that her boss insisted she take control of her team by changing their sales approach and cleaning up problems left by the previous manager. She resisted the urge to tell them what to do, and instead spent time observing them, understanding their routines and learning about the business. She used an external coach to discuss her insecurities about being a new manager, and to get herself out of their way. Instead of micromanaging, she directed her energy to finding out what employees loved about their jobs and how to make their jobs more interesting. This positive inquiry transformed the team energy, creating an environment that engaged and energized, resulting in fulfilled and satisfied employees producing extraordinary results. The positive energy became contagious and spread to other sales teams and organizations within the company. **«**

Tapping into an employee's self-sustaining and positive energy source, and then getting yourself out of the way, is the key to long-term effectiveness and satisfaction. Amazingly, this simple strategy often makes the job of leading easier.

Be a Catalyst for Waking Others Up

Leaders can achieve extraordinary results by tapping into the often-ignored energy derived from physical, emotional, spiritual and relational sources. Making sure employees are awake, energized and engaged can produce powerful outcomes that will transcend those produced from traditional management methods.

The job of leading is a paradox. On one hand, it has become harder because the key to effectiveness has shifted away from being an intellectual expert. On the other hand, leadership that nurtures passion, promotes effective relationships and embraces emotional expression, is intuitive and relatively simple. The bottom line is that leaders who learn how to redirect energy in their organizations, and who utilize both the economic and emotional elements, are more likely to be positively impacting the workplace energy crisis.

> *If businesses are to grow their way out of the current economic malaise,*
> *they will have to get more productivity out of their people—not by*
> *cutting and slashing, but by nurturing, engaging and recognizing.*
>
> John Byrne, *Fast Company*, August 2003

It is time for leaders to focus on their own passion as a source of energy, and to embrace and cultivate the unique qualities and energy sources of their employees. In doing so, they will create an atmosphere where the human spirit can thrive.

Gina Lavery

Gina Lavery helps leaders discover and utilize their passion to create environments that support the human spirit. She is a writer, speaker and global leadership consultant with two decades of international and managerial experience. Prior to establishing her successful consulting practice, Gina spent the majority of her career with Abbott Laboratories, a Fortune 100 healthcare company, where she focused on organization development, sales management, product management, advertising, sales and auditing.

Gina brings real-world perspective to her clients through her experiences in line management and global settings—she has lived, worked and studied in 38 countries around the globe. As a consultant, her specialties include executive coaching and development, team facilitation and development, design and delivery of experiential training and employee motivation and engagement. Her client list includes Allstate Life Insurance Company, ABN AMRO, Abbott Laboratories, Blood Centers of America, Metadynamics, Inc. and the Robert L. Bosch Corporation.

Gina holds a Master's degree in Organization Development from the Executive Program of the George L. Graziadio School of Business and Management at Pepperdine University. Her master's degree thesis studied the relationship between emotional intelligence and career engagement.

Business Name:	Synchronicity Partners
Address:	1445 West Belden #4M, Chicago, IL USA 60614
Telephone:	773-935-7629
Fax:	773-935-9956
E-mail:	ginalavery@yahoo.com
Professional Affiliations:	Organization Development Network; International Coach Federation; Pepperdine MSOD Alumni Network; Human Resources Management Association of Chicago.

Clare Mann

Clare Mann Associates, trading as The Myths of Life

Work–Life Integration: The New Paradigm

Research into work–life balance has increased as organizations and the individuals within them ponder ways in which they can improve their quality of life, while simultaneously being viable and productive. Many of us question the imbalances we experience in our lives. We have become concerned about the increasing amount of time spent at work and its impact on our families and our health. Some of us are fearful of events, such as family holidays: On the one hand, we may feel we have lost autonomy over many of our basic non-work relationships—perhaps our children won't listen to us; on the other hand, we are anxious about what is happening back in the office.

As many organizational consultants will testify, conversations with executives often reveal concerns, not about strategies or performance management, but generally about the imbalance between their work and other aspects of their lives. This trend requires a radical reappraisal of how we live our lives, since for many of us, work appears to take too great a proportion of our energy. Often, it is not until family demands increase or change across our lifespan, aged parents become more dependent, or retirement looms, that we ask, "How can I make changes to my life now to ensure I live an integrated and well-lived life?"

Improved work–life balance appears to hold the promise of a reprieve as we seek satisfaction in both work and non-work activities. Sadly, a focus on creating greater work–life balance often focuses upon time management as we seek to apportion our time between the disparate areas of our lives. We consider the 168 hours we have every week and try to rebalance how we spread ourselves across our numerous roles and commitments.

However, is improved work–life balance the answer? I suggest it isn't. Firstly, we only have one life, despite dividing our time between work and non-work activities, and apportioning time between work and personal life forces us into separation and fragmentation. Secondly, it implies that greater time management will result in expending effort productively across the different parts of our life. Lack of time, however, is a red herring in the work–life balance debate—it results in us relinquishing responsibility for the real choices facing us in creating the life we want to live. The solution lies in discovering what is really important, meaningful and significant to us. It requires a reconsideration of the quality of our life—not our work life, home life or family life, but the quality of this one thing that we call *life*.

Shifting the Paradigm

The word "balance" implies some sort of see-saw, with work on one side and family and personal life on the other. Like scales of justice, it suggests that both sides are equal. It implies constantly juggling to maintain balance, with sudden or increased demand on one side throwing the other side precariously out of balance. One problem is that "work–life balance" is deeply embedded in our language, and every time we see the word *balance* it reinforces the balancing act.

Changing your paradigm starts with changing your language. I want to encourage you, in considering your own balancing act or, if applicable, those of the people in your organization, to change the concept to *work–life integration*. Here you move away from the see-saw to see that it is not the only option in the playground. Work–life integration implies a synergy between the different aspects of your life, whereby energy is expended more productively. It implies that you and the organization in which you work can have your cake and eat it too!

In an endeavor to create improved work–life integration, you might discover that the organization or profession in which you operate resists the change this inevitably involves. Often the argument is that it is not viable and doesn't make business sense. Fortunately, when organizations transform their operations to create work–life integration, it reflects positively in the bottom line, and employees feel better about their lives and the role that work plays in them. For example, AT&T in the early 1990s conducted an experiment involving 100,000 people, from the CEO to phone operators, to explore how the organization could transform the workplace by moving the work to the worker rather than the other way around. Since 1991, AT&T has freed up some $550 million US in cash flow—a 30 percent improvement—by eliminating offices people don't need, consolidating others, and reducing related overhead costs.

Similarly, IBM is saving more than $100 million US annually in its North American sales and distribution unit alone, due to workplace flexibility set out in its Mobility Initiative. In addition, a survey of employees in this initiative revealed that 87 percent believe that their personal productivity and effectiveness on the job have increased significantly.

Diane Halpern and Susan Murphy, in their 2005 book *From Work-Family BALANCE to Work-Family INTERACTION: Changing the Metaphor*, indicate that these examples and other studies show that these initiatives to create options for combining work and personal life effectively result in foundations being laid for individuals to build richer and fuller lives. These studies indicate that when an organization gets work–life integration right, it doesn't merely produce a warm feeling—it positively affects the bottom line and, ultimately, the share value of the corporation.

Work–life integration is about combining work and personal life, including family, children and personal growth, in ways that are mutually supporting. Work and personal life are *not* two independent spheres of life. The debate on work–life integration involves employers and working families (in whatever form) understanding the work–life options available. Thus choices can be made that offer returns-on-investments to employers, families and society at large which are consistent with personal and societal values—a challenging but, I believe, achievable goal.

The Business Case for Work–Life Integration

Despite resistance by many organizations combining work and personal life in mutually rewarding ways, many companies have succeeded in finding a *third* option—changing their organizations to what is known as the Alternative

Workplace. This is the combination of non-traditional work practices, settings and locations that supplement traditional offices. For example, when Dow Chemical transitioned into a virtual organization by turning to telework, it reduced its field support operations from 21 offices in 1990 to eight in 1995. By 1999, one sales administration center remained in North America with support departments moved to their Michigan headquarters. Creating a virtual sales force was about more than just sending 500 salespeople home to work. It was about transforming culture, work habits and technology and ensuring a team of traditional workers transitioned into a virtual organization without losing their way or damaging the company's sales and customer relationships. In short, it was about change management, and it made business sense too. In terms of the bottom line, administrative costs dropped 50 percent annually and productivity increased by 32.5 percent. Ten percent of this was achieved through decreased absenteeism, 16 percent by working at home, and 6.5 percent by employees avoiding the commute. Telework offered individuals increased flexibility in terms of where, how and when they worked, and it meant that work and family commitments became complementary.

Another example is British Telecom, which transformed its business operation from a more static, office-based workforce to "e-BT" to service its 21 million customers. Redesigning work, whereby employees have on-line, real-time access to information, not only increased productivity but also increased sales, customer satisfaction and flexible working for *all* employees. BT now has 7,000 home workers, 650 job sharers and 6,600 part-time workers and:

- a more talented, flexible and responsive workforce drawn from a larger pool;
- reduced natural attrition of only 3 percent of the workforce;
- £3 Million ($5 million US) savings in recruitment and induction costs as 98 percent of women return after maternity leave;
- absenteeism down to 3.1 percent, compared to the UK average of 8.5 percent;
- 31 percent increase in productivity in those 7,000 home workers;
- a savings of £53M ($94 million US) per year, since it costs £2,000 ($3,500 US) to set up a home worker, while each desk not used saves £6,000 ($10,500 US) per annum.

These examples show that addressing work–life integration makes business sense, as well as promoting improved morale, lowered turnover, increased staff retention and employee commitment. Other companies, such as Eli Lilly Pharmaceuticals, AT&T and Sainsbury's in the UK, are also implementing creative ways to improve bottom-line performance, while increasing satisfaction and choice for all employees.

Friedman, Christensen & De Groot in *Integrating Work and Life: The Wharton Resource Guide* (1998) showed that family-friendly policies arising out of these decisions *do* mean that people spend less time working, but that there is *no* negative impact on productivity since people work smarter. Additionally, organizations benefit from the increased commitment of workers and lower staff turnover because organizations consider them as whole people, not just human resources.

Enabling Change

If you are in a position to make such changes, you may be asking, "How do I do this in my organization?" Ricardo Semler, CEO of SEMCO, made the kind of radical changes that organizations like IBM, General Motors, Ford, Kodak and Nestlés have tried to learn from. In his 1993 book *Maverick! The success story behind the world's most unusual workplace,* Semler talks of his deteriorating company—with diminishing profits, low morale, burnout and lack of initiative and creativity.

Work–life changes in SEMCO began with Semler leading the way by reducing his own working hours and changing his philosophy on the quality of life and the intrinsic value of people. *This is absolutely essential.* Friedman & Greenhaus, in *Work and Family—Allies or Enemies? What happens when business professionals confront life choices* (2000), reported that in companies with family-friendly policies, there remains little take-up if managers only play lip service to work–life integration.

A report in the *Harvard Review 2000* on work–life balance indicates that many organizations, including AT&T and IBM, are pioneering the Alternative Workplace. This is *not* a fad. It is probably safe to say that some 30 to 40 million people in the US are now either telecommuters or home-based workers. The authors of the report indicate that three principles guide these new managers who are trying to collaborate to achieve work and personal objectives for everyone's benefits:

1. Employees must be made aware of business priorities and encouraged to be clear about their *own* personal priorities;

2. There must be recognition and support for employees as whole people with a celebration of their roles at home and at work;

3. Creative approaches to work that enhance the organization's performance, as well as allowing employees to pursue their own goals, must be considered.

Clearly there is a business case for work–life integration, with the perspective shifting from the juggling act of work–life balance to creating a context for an integrated and fulfilling life. What are the personal barriers that inhibit us from seeking alternative ways to create the lives we truly desire within our own particular set of circumstances?

Barriers to Change

It can be overwhelming to consider the organizational changes that must precipitate an individual creating a truly integrated life. However, real change can start with one person making changes to their own life. This can have an amazing ripple effect as others witness the renewed energy and enthusiasm that results from living a fully integrated life. What changes can you make today to ensure that the different aspects of your life are complementary and rewarding? The first step is to consider the barriers that stand in the way of you making the changes necessary for personal and professional fulfillment.

The following list describes 10 of the barriers that may inhibit us from seeking alternative ways to create the lives we truly desire.

1. We deny that we have the freedom to change. Anticipating change can become so overwhelming that to reduce the anxiety of choosing, we deny that we have any choice at all. The crux of freedom is realizing that you are the captain of your mind and are free to think in whatever way you want. To avoid the anxiety inherent in choosing is to lead a life dictated by others of which you are only a passive observer.

2. We lose sight of what inspires us to reach for the impossible. Our everyday commitments both at work and at home often become so onerous that we might believe that our vision of a rich and fulfilling life is mere fantasy. This is only the case if we allow it. We can redefine a clear vision of how work and personal life can be truly integrated if only we believe it.

3. We believe we have no right to mastery over our own lives. Often, social pressures influence us to believe that we have to do certain things because someone else decrees it. However, we don't have to do anything because someone else dictates it. If we do these things, it is because we choose to do them. Even if they feel like obligations, they are still choices and we must take responsibility for them.

4. We lack the energy to make changes and learn new things. It is all too easy to become stifled and weighed down with duty and routine. To consider changing our life situation then becomes too threatening. We ask "Who would I be without my job? My current relationship? My status? What would happen if I no longer earned the income I have worked so hard to secure?" Instead of feeling safe and strong, we feel stifled, resentful or just plain bored. Change begins with daring to address the issues that underpin our current and future choices and living with the anxiety that meaningful living entails.

5. We continue with earlier choices out of a sense of duty and obligation. Sometimes, our roles and responsibilities appear to weigh us down and we forget that we too have a responsibility to ourselves. By regaining mastery over the way in which we live our lives, we can integrate our responsibilities to others with respect for ourselves. In turn, we become role models to our children and peers of the importance of taking responsibilities for the choices we make.

6. We resist the anxiety that results from relinquishing alternative choices. In choosing to change our lives, we inevitably are faced with the dilemma of turning down alternative courses of action. Although the anxiety of our freedom accompanies all new decisions, we must accept that this is a part of a well-lived life.

Embracing anxiety allows us to apply caution where necessary and avoid the stagnation and resentment inherent in *not* choosing.

7. We fear the judgment of others whose lives may be affected by our decisions. Often, changing our lives can be threatening to others, some of whom are affected by our decisions and some of who are unsettled by how we are changing. Often, the anticipation of others' judgments is greater than the manifestation of them and to not choose is to court anger and resentment in ourselves and others.

8. We relinquish responsibility for our own lives, instead blaming others for our predicament. If we choose not to choose, events will transpire to bring about changes to our lives. When this happens, it is all too easy to blame others for our predicament, believing that we would have acted differently had the circumstances been different. However, we cannot relinquish responsibility for our own lives, even if we allow others to choose for us.

9. We hold steadfastly to a sense of safety that results from maintaining the status quo. As we make decisions, a sense of safety or duty inhibits our willingness to embrace new possibilities. Although it is seductive to continue on a path we believed would bring us happiness, it is important to re-evaluate our lives *now* to assess the extent to which our choices are delivering the rewards we expect from an integrated life.

10. We become prey to the Identity Myth. The Identity Myth is the belief that you should be someone other than the person you want to be, or that fitting with others' expectations and desires will bring you happiness. This belief is so pervasive that it requires fuller explanation of the way in which it influences our lives and the potential for an integrated life.

The Identity Myth

The Identity Myth relates to all aspects of our existence and implies that we are unduly influenced by others' expectations and demands and somehow out of touch with the myriad of choices and options available to us. Those influences come from personal, social and cultural expectations and are often subtle, resulting in us believing we don't have any choice at all. In relation to work–life integration, it implies that these influences are so strong that we allow fashion, consensus, culture and social expectations to choose for us. We might thus believe that work as we experience it now—the linear career of nine-to-five and beyond, five days a week in a physical location—is the only option. It also implies that the balancing act inherent in work–life balance holds its own solution. For instance, one has to focus on one or the other. Life-shifters, down-shifters and sea-changers choose one side, and those committed to career and corporate success choose the other.

This limited perspective inhibits the possibility of real change for both individuals and organizations. If the Identity Myth influences you to such an extent that you have very fixed views of how you should be in both work and non-work roles, you need to broaden your perspective to capture all the elements you want. This will enable you to develop the life you truly want to live, not one dictated to you by unquestioned stereotypes, culture, socialization and your own limiting beliefs. It is a myth that you must forego your health and well-being to achieve success in the corporate environment. It is also untrue that you must forego a successful career if you want to commit to a fulfilling family and personal life. What is required is a paradigm shift from seeing yourself as a collection of disparate roles and commitments to a holistic, integrated person.

Beliefs Underlying Our Choices

Numerous beliefs underpin the choices we face for developing an integrated life. These beliefs are both perpetuated and reinforced by the social context in which we live and the organizational culture within which we work. Beliefs are unquestioned assumptions that are rarely challenged but hoodwink us into believing that we have less choice than we do. Beliefs impinge on the practices we develop in our *own* lives and the policies developed in our organizations. When we anticipate changes in our lives, we often become immobilized by the many assumptions and fears that arise. The following examples illustrate these fears and highlight the underpinning beliefs that must be addressed if we are to reclaim mastery over our lives:

- It's not the organization's responsibility to consider my personal life;
- Commitment to family and personal issues reduce career focus;
- You have to do long hours to get ahead and be promoted;
- People will think I am lazy or weak if I don't put in 110 percent;
- People will not understand me—they will think me soft and losing my edge.

Now before we explore ways in which we can fully realize our freedom and its implications for a more integrated lifestyle, we need to be clear about our own beliefs and assumptions.

Exercise #1

Consider your personal work–life balance. What are your beliefs and assumptions about combining work and personal life in a more integrated manner?

Bear these beliefs in mind as you consider the following section, remembering that your own assumptions fuel your actions and will facilitate or sabotage any changes you will make towards an integrated lifestyle.

Creating a Truly Integrated Life

At this stage, you may ask, "How can I change when I have so many responsibilities?" Change begins by questioning the myths underpinning your behavior and embracing the anxiety that inevitably accompanies adjustment. Change also causes anxiety, so it is valuable to develop a strategy to identify what is important to you and a vision for the integrated life you so desire. The following exercise will help you determine what is really right for you and envision how to attain the life you really desire.

Exercise #2

Imagine you are free to create an integrated life in whatever form you want. Write down exactly what this would look like. The two paragraphs following this exercise may be helpful in doing this, so refer to them first.

Be as creative as you want in choosing what you would do. Remember that this is your ideal. Don't be put off by thinking it would be impossible to achieve. At this stage you can live your dream on paper. Remember that you can't change others, but you can imagine what it would be like to have people in your life that you spend time with because you really want to. Of course, you may include people and things in your ideal life that you already have. Don't include anything or anyone only because you can't imagine what it would be like without them.

Write down as much detail as possible, and when you have finished, close your eyes and imagine yourself living that life. Carry this image around with you for the next few weeks and at regular times reflect on it. After a while a core image will probably emerge. It will represent the focus around which your ideal life is centered. Make a note of this—it will help you with the next step.

Exercise #3

Consider what will be entailed in achieving your dream and note this in detail.

- Requirements:
- Time:
- Resources:
- Knowledge:
- Money:
- Personal costs:
- Emotional support:

It is very tempting to modify your dream because it seems impossible, given your present circumstances. Try to avoid this, since you will never be happy unless you have a clear picture of what you want.

Exercise #4

What would it take to achieve your dream? What is the shortfall between your dream and your current lifestyle?

Completing these exercises will enable you to gain clarity about the integrated life you want. Through this process, you will also have highlighted ways in which your beliefs might inhibit or facilitate you changing your current lifestyle. By identifying the beliefs you might have to change and with a new vision for the future, you are equipped to appraise the options available to you to achieve it.

There are three likely strategies available to achieve greater work–life integration:

1. Seeking an organization that enables you to integrate the lifestyle choices you desire;

2. Leaving the traditional organizational environment and becoming self-employed, thereby increasing your autonomy and flexibility; or

3. Developing ways in which you can negotiate a more integrated life with your existing employer.

To assist you in deciding the relative merits of these choices, it is valuable to assess the extent to which your own beliefs and desires about an integrated lifestyle are aligned with that of your existing or desired workplace. This can be done by completing a short on-line questionnaire to ascertain both your organization's and your own commitment to work–life integration. This questionnaire can be found at www.MythOfWorkLifeBalance.com and will assist you in choosing the next best course of action.

To improve the quality of your life and gain satisfaction from both work and non-work activities, it is essential to uncover the myths or unquestioned assumptions that fuel your current behavior. This requires a paradigm shift from the juggling act of work–life balance to the satisfying and fulfilling option of work–life integration. This requires re-evaluating your options, challenging limiting beliefs and myths, and creating a lifestyle that is sustainable. Managements that celebrate this reality are reaping the benefits in bottom-line performance, at the same time creating organizations that are satisfying communities in which to work.

If you choose to make changes in your personal life, I believe you will see that the issue is greater than one of individual choice or individual organizational policy. We must ask, "What sort of society do we want to create and what do we want the organizations of the future to look like? Is it sustainable to continue as we are?" work–life integration and the alternative workplace will, thus, become hot topics for the future.

Clare Mann

Clare Mann is an Organizational Psychologist and Existential Psychotherapist with extensive international experience including work–life integration, management development, executive coaching and change management. Her corporate experience led her to re-evaluate her own work–life integration. She now focuses on creative approaches to work–life integration for organizational transformation.

Prior to holding a Senior Lectureship in Occupational Psychology in a British university, Clare was a human resources manager. She developed open learning provision internationally and chaired a team responsible for quality standards in HRM. Following changes in the British National Health Service, she became Chief External Examiner on the BSc/Diploma in Health Services Management for the Royal College of Nursing.

Clare co-authored *Strategic Human Resource Development*, 2005 (ISBN 0750662506) and is the author of *The Myths of Life and the Choices We Have*, 2005 (ISBN 0646441752). She now offers consultancy, professional speaking, workshops, books and resources on work–life integration and the alternative workplace.

Business Name:	Clare Mann Associates
Address:	Suite 101, 30 Foveaux Street,
	Surry Hills, NSW 2010 Australia
Telephone:	+61 2 9713 8612
Fax:	+61 2 8569 1384
E-mail:	info@lifemyths.com
Web Address:	www.mythofworklifebalance.com
	www.lifemyths.com
Professional Affiliations:	British and Australian Psychological Society; Australian Institute of Management; United Kingdom Council of Psychotherapists; Universities Council of Psychotherapists and Counsellors

Kathy Glover Scott, M.S.W.

Kathy Glover Scott is a multi-dimensional speaker and executive coach with the power to transform. Kathy teaches and weaves together best business practices with advanced energy work to help attain powerful results. She is not only the co-publisher of this series, Kathy is the author of the internationally acclaimed *Esteem!,* and *The Successful Woman* (also published in Europe and Asia). She is in demand as a 'cutting edge' keynote speaker and leader in innovative energy practices.

She is only one of three people in North America accepted to teach Reiki to the 21st degree, as well as other advanced energy based courses. Visit her website for speaking topics, online courses and upcoming programs in your area.

Books and CDs by Kathy Glover Scott:

- The Successful Woman
- The Craft of Writing for Speakers (CD)
- Expert Women Who Speak...Speak Out! (co-editor/publisher)
  Volume 1 (2002), Volume 2 (2003), Volume 3 (2003),
  Volume 4 (2004), Volume 5 (2005)
- Sales Gurus Speak Out (co-editor/publisher)
- Esteem! A Powerful Guide to Living the Life You Deserve!

Business Name:	Kathy Glover Scott & Associates
Address:	P.O. Box 72073, Kanata North RPO
	Kanata, ON K2K 2P4
Telephone:	613-271-8636
E-mail:	Kathy@kathygloverscott.com
Web Address:	www.kathygloverscott.com
Professional Affiliations:	International Federation of Professional Speakers, Canadian Association of Professional Speakers (Ottawa Chapter, Professional Member)

Adele Alfano

Canada's Diamond Coach **Adele Alfano** is known nationally as an inspiring speaker, heart-warming keynoter, informative seminar leader, co-publisher and author. She has earned the reputation of being a "mining" expert in human potential and personal empowerment. Renowned for her proven techniques, she has helped hundreds of people capitalize on their unique abilities to maximize their potential. This makes her a popular choice by many organizations, meeting planners and speakers bureaus such as the National Speakers Bureau.

As a professional member with the Canadian Association of Professional Speakers (CAPS), she has enjoyed the status of being one of the founding members and past president of the Hamilton Chapter. Her sparkling signature stories have made her a popular contributor to magazines, and guest at health shows, trade shows and on women's radio programs. One of her own sparkling moments was being nominated for Woman of the Year in Hamilton in 1998.

Her monthly newsletter, "Spread the Sparkle," has been well-received all over the world. She is also the founder of the consistently sold-out "fun"-raising events in Southwestern Ontario called "Kiss my Tiara!"

Along with her business partner Kathy Glover Scott, Adele is also the co-editor and co-publisher of collaborative books entitled Expert Women Who Speak…Speak Out! In this first-ever series, Canadian professional women speakers and experts in their fields have come together to share their collective wisdom and female perspective on life.

Business Name:	Diamond Within Resources: Speaking and Consulting
Address:	P.O. Box 60511, Mountain Plaza P. O.,
	Hamilton ON L9C 7N7
Telephone:	905-578-6687
Fax:	905-578-6687 (call first)
E-mail:	adele@diamondwithin.com
Web Address:	www.AdeleAlfano.com
	www.kissmytiara.ca
Professional Affiliations:	Professional member of the Canadian Association
	of Professional Speakers

Experts Who Speak Books

With this sixth volume in the **Experts Who Speak** book series, we are firmly established as an influential forum to globally promote professional speakers and trainers and provide them with the opportunity to be best-selling authors. If you are in the public eye and speaking, training or coaching is your field of endeavor, you may be interested in joining us. Our upcoming titles include:

- Sales Gurus Speak Out, Volume 2
- Internet Gurus Speak Out
- Marketing Gurus Speak Out

• • •

**Follow your dreams with intention and
passion and let the amazing journey unfold.**

• • •

*Kathy Glover Scott and Adele Alfano,
Publishers of Experts Who Speak Books*

For more information on upcoming volumes,
or how to be a contributor, please contact either:

**Adele Alfano www.diamondwithin.com
or
Kathy Glover Scott www.kathygloverscott.com**

**Visit our websites:
www.expertswhospeakbooks.com
www.expertwomenspeakout.com
www.salesgurusspeakout.com
www.awakeningtheworkplace.com**

Thanks to Creative Bound International Inc.
for assisting us in making this best-selling series a reality.
www.creativebound.com